The Massey Lectures Series

The Massey Lectures are co-sponsored by Massey College, in the University of Toronto, and CBC Radio. The series was created in honour of the Right Honourable Vincent Massey, former governor general of Canada, and was inaugurated in 1961 to enable distinguished authorities to communicate the results of original study or research on important subjects of contemporary interest.

This book comprises the 1993 Massey Lectures, "Democracy on Trial," which were first broadcast in November–December 1993 as part of CBC Radio's *Ideas* series. The executive producer of the series was Bernie Lucht.

ALSO BY JEAN BETHKE ELSHTAIN

*Public Man, Private Woman: Women in Social and
Political Thought*   1981

The Family in Political Thought   1982

Meditations on Modern Political Thought   1986

Women and War   1987

Power Trips and Other Journeys   1990

Co-author

*But Was It Just: Reflections on the Morality
of the Persian Gulf War,* with Michael Walzer,
George Weigel, Stanley Hauerwas,
and Sari Nusseibeh   1992

Editor

Just War Theory   1990

Co-editor

Women, Militarism, and the Arms Race   1990

*Rebuilding the Nest: A New Commitment to the
American Family*   1990

DEMOCRACY ON TRIAL

JEAN BETHKE ELSHTAIN

Published in 1993 by
House of Anansi Press Limited
1800 Steeles Avenue West
Concord, Ontario
L4K 2P3
(416) 445-3333

Second printing October 1996

CBC logo used by permission

Canadian Cataloguing in Publication Data

Elshtain, Jean Bethke, 1941–
Democracy on trial

(CBC Massey Lectures Series; 1993)
ISBN 0-88784-545-2

1. Democracy.   I. title.
II. Series: Massey lectures.

JC421.E57 1993   321.8   C93-095231-6

Cover Design: Brant Cowie/ArtPlus Limited
Cover Photograph: Kunio Owaki/Masterfile
Typesetting: Tony Gordon Ltd.

Printed and bound in Canada

*House of Anansi Press gratefully acknowledges the
support of the Canada Council and the Ontario Arts Council
in the development of writing and publishing in Canada.*

For my friends in Prague who taught me much about the drama of democracy, and whose new democracy is itself on trial, especially Jana Krchová and David Krch. Thanks also to Vladimira Záková for genial company and translation. Martin Palous has been a fascinating interlocutor on matters political and philosophical, both in Prague and in the United States. Ivan Havel and Josef Vavroušek have been gracious and helpful. Michaela Freiová gave generously of her time in order to discuss problems of women and politics and refugee matters. The Prague Mothers shared their homes and information. My special gratitude goes to Václav Havel for his example as a performer of political thought, a powerful guide through the drama of democratic possibilities and perils as the twentieth century nears its end. Finally, to J.D.D. for friendship's sake and for being such a trouper.

Contents

Acknowledgements ix

I   Democracy's Precarious Present *1*

II   Democracy and the Politics of Displacement *35*

III   Democracy and the Politics of Difference *63*

IV   Democracy's Shady Past *91*

V   Democracy's Enduring Promise *117*

Notes *143*

Acknowledgements

THIS BOOK FIRST SAW the light of day as part of the 1993 Massey Lectures I was invited and honoured to give in the fall of that year. Special thanks to Bernie Lucht, executive producer of CBC Radio's *Ideas*, Jill Eisen for keeping me on track, Jamie Swift, who first had the idea, and Michael Carroll for excellent editing. Ann Saddlemyer, master of Massey College, was a gracious hostess.

I
DEMOCRACY'S PRECARIOUS PRESENT

NO ONE CAN SAY we live in uninteresting times! Even as nations and peoples formerly under the domination of the Soviet empire proclaim their political ideals in language that inspired and secured the founding of Western democracies; even as Russia herself, and the various successor states springing up in the wreckage of the terrible Soviet system, flail toward democracy or run away from it, our own democracy — I speak here as an American — is faltering, not flourishing. More and more, we Americans confront one another as aggrieved groups rather than as free citizens. In this first chapter I will explore flash points in established democracies with the American experiment as my chief example. The trials and tribulations of the American republic have a way of setting the agenda for other democratic societies, whether for good or for ill. In speaking about my own country I will refer to Western democracies more generally much of the time.

How will the drama of democracy be played out in the twenty-first century? Are we citizens of Western democracies, in fact, in the danger zone? The signs of the times are not encouraging. The perils facing our democracy are many. They include deepening cynicism, the growth of corrosive forms of individualism and statism, the loss of civil society. Democracy requires laws and constitutional procedures, yes, but it also depends on the everyday actions and spirit of the people. On that ground — we are in trouble. We have a veritable shopping list of disconcerting facts at our disposal that speaks to cynicism and a turn inward toward the self.

Many political commentators in the United States write of the growth of a "culture of mistrust," aided and abetted by scandals, a press that feeds off scandals, and a public that seems insatiable in its appetite for scandal. The culture of mistrust fuels declining levels of involvement in politics and stokes cynicism about politics and politicians. Journalist E. J. Dionne's book *Why Americans Hate Politics* offers a strong story of what has gone awry. According to Dionne, both liberals and conservatives are failing America. He laments in particular a false polarization in American politics that is more and more cast in the form of a cultural civil war. One sees, first, liberal Democrats who wish to tame the logic of the market in economic life but allow a nearly untrammelled laissez-faire in cultural and sexual life where individual rights are trumps. Their mirror image is provided by conservative Republicans who offer a story of constraints and controls in the cultural and sexual sphere but embrace a nearly unconstrained market.[1] Politics and citizens get stuck in the *danse macabre* of these two logics and see no clear way out.

A second perceptive analysis of America's recent political travail is *Chain Reaction*, an account by Thomas Byrne Edsall and Mary D. Edsall of "the impact of race, rights, and taxes on American Politics."[2] The Edsalls unpack a conundrum that will not go away anytime soon. Theirs is a story of how, over the years, numerous programs targeted specifically at black and underclass Americans lost legitimacy. Preferential hiring programs, for example, provoke deep resentment and stoke racial divisions. Aid to dependent children and similar programs appear to sustain, even encourage, an out-of-wedlock birth rate running around seventy percent of all births to inner-city mothers, many of them teenagers.

Those who have paid most of the bills, being the majority — lower-middle-class and middle-class whites — no longer see a benefit flowing from such programs to the society as a whole (as evidence mounts about growing welfare dependency, inner-city crime, and the like) but perceive, instead, a pattern of redistribution through forms of assistance to people who do not appear to be as committed as they are to following the rules of the game, by working hard and not expecting government to shoulder their burdens. This, at least, is a widespread conviction. As a result, programs geared to particular populations have lost the legitimacy accorded almost automatically to inclusive programs such as Social Security. Despite their unpopularity, policies that target groups on racial, gender, or sexual preference grounds are difficult to alter given a phenomenon called "clientele capture." This means, simply, that a small number of vocal clients of such policies have a vested interest in preventing change, even though, over the long run, their own cause loses the support of the vast majority of their fellow citizens.

These and other examples of disaffection speak to a deeper matter, which I already noted briefly. The "loss of civil society" lies in the background to our current discontents, helping to account for why democracy itself is going through an ordeal of self-understanding as we near the end of the century. It is through the associational enthusiasms of civil society that the democratic ethos and spirit of citizens have been made manifest. By civil society I mean the many forms of community and association that dot the landscape of a democratic culture, from families to churches to neighbourhood associations to trade unions to self-help movements to volunteer assistance to the needy. This network lies outside the formal structure of state power. Democratic observers have long recognized the vital importance of civil society. Some have spoken of "mediating institutions," structures between the individual and the government or state. These mediating institutions located the child, for example, in his or her little estate, the family, which was itself nested within a wider, overlapping framework of sustaining and supporting civic institutions — churches, schools, voluntary associations of all kinds, solidaristic organizations such as unions or mothers' groups. American society was honeycombed by a vast network that offered a sustaining social ecology for the growing citizen.

Curiously the framers of the American Constitution paid little explicit attention to such institutions. Perhaps the framers did not mention the associations of civil society, including the family, because they simply assumed their vitality and longevity. They counted on a social deposit of intergenerational trust, neighbourliness, and civic responsibility. But we no longer can. That is why political theorists, of whom I am one, must tend explicitly to this matter. For we see the ill effect of a loss of civil society all around us.

Think, if you will and if you can bear it, of the growing number of American children for whom neither home nor street nor neighbourhood affords a safe haven. More and more American children grow up frightened, and increasing numbers are scarred by violence in schools and streets. Now we know certain things. The data is overwhelming and consistent. We know that the strongest predictors of situations in which children are abused are single-parent households, or households with an unmarried couple (often a biological mother and her children living with a male unrelated to those children either by birth or by acceptance of legal responsibility for their well-being). Undersupervised foster-care situations are another predictor. We further know that a stable, two-parent household is the best protection not only against child abuse but against the possibility that a child himself or herself will grow up to be an abuser.

Fully seventy percent of juveniles in state reform institutions grew up in homes with a serious parental deficit, as the sociologists like to call it. I refer to domestic circumstances with fewer helping hands than necessary and less than adequate emotional, economic, and social support. Beyond the tragedy of children assaulted in their homes, an astonishing number die from violence — especially gun violence. Homicide by firearms is now the second leading cause of death for fifteen- to nineteen-year-old white Americans (after motor vehicle accidents). For black Americans in the same age bracket, homicide is the leading cause of death. Over the long run, stemming the tide of family collapse is the best protection against being either the victim or the perpetrator of violence. But families cannot do this alone. They need neighbours to turn to, churches to give not only solace but solid, hands-on help, a network of friends, agencies that assist in a time of trouble such as a serious, prolonged illness, and so on. That socially rich world is the world of civil society. If we are to sustain our democratic culture, we depend on civil society.

Note that civil society is a realm that is neither individualist nor collectivist. It partakes of both the "I" and the "we." Here I think of the many lodges and clubs and party precinct organizations that once dotted the American landscape. It is that world of small-scale *civitate* that is evoked by the Anti-Federalists in debates over ratification of the United States Constitution. The Anti-Federalists were not as confident as the Federalists about the long-term survival of robust civic bodies, and they hoped to make provision for their flourishing. No doubt these Anti-Federalists pushed an idealized image of a self-reliant republic that shunned imperial power and worked, instead, to create a polity modelled on classic principles of civic virtue and a common good. As Ralph Ketcham, a historian of this argument, writes:

> Anti-federalists saw mild, grass-roots, small-scale governments in sharp contrast to the splendid edifice and overweening ambitions implicit in the new Constitution. . . . The first left citizens free to live their own lives and to cultivate the virtue (private and public) vital to republicanism, while the second soon entailed taxes and drafts and offices and wars damaging to human dignity and thus fatal to self-government.[3]

Despite the often roseate hue with which the Anti-Federalists surrounded their arguments, they were onto something, as we like to say. They hoped to avoid, even to break, a cycle later elaborated by Alexis de Tocqueville in his great work, *Democracy in America*. Tocqueville sketched as a warning a world in decline, a world different from the robust democracy he surveyed. He believed American democratic citizens needed to take to heart a possible corruption of their way of life. In his worst-case scenario, narrowly self-interested individualists, disarticulated from the saving constraints and nurture of overlapping associations of social life, required more and

more controls "from above" in order that the disin-
tegrative effects of untrammelled individualism of
this bad sort be at least somewhat muted in practice.

To this end, he cautioned, the peripheries must
remain vital; political spaces other than or beneath
those of the state needed to be cherished, nourished,
kept vibrant. Tocqueville had in mind local councils
and committees in order to forestall concentrations
of power at the core or on the top. Too much centralized power was as bad as no power at all. Only
small-scale *civitates* would enable individuals, as citizens, to cultivate democratic virtues and possibilities, to play an active role in the drama of democracy.
Such participation turns on meaningful involvement
in some form of community. Too much power exercised at a level beyond that which permits and
encourages active citizen participation is destructive of civic dignity and, finally, fatal to any authentic understanding of democratic self-government.
Anti-Federalist fears of centralized power presaged
Tocqueville's worries that imperial greatness
bought through force of arms is "pleasing to the
imagination of a democratic people" because it
sends out lightning bolts of "vivid and sudden lus-
ter, obtained without toil, by nothing but the risk of
life."[4]

Tocqueville's worries have been much debated by
political and social theorists. Those who follow
Tocqueville in this matter believe that the reality of
American democracy freed individuals from the
constraints of older, undemocratic structures and
obligations. But, at the same time, individualism

and privatization were also unleashed. Tocqueville's fear was not that this invites anarchy, as antidemocratic philosophers like Plato and Thomas Hobbes insisted; rather, he believed that the individualism of an acquisitive commercial republic would engender new forms of social and political domination. He called this bad form of individualism "egoism" in order to distinguish it from the notion of human dignity and self-responsibility central to a flourishing democratic way of life. All social webs that once held persons intact having disintegrated, the individual finds himself or herself isolated and impotent, exposed and unprotected. Into this power vacuum moves the organized force of government in the form of a top-heavy, centralized state. I will say more about this Tocquevillian anxiety where the state is concerned in a moment but, first, consider several additional criticisms, even indictments, of the contemporary Western, democratic way of life.

Keep in mind the concern, namely, that over time the stripping down of the individual to a hard core of an isolated or suspended self, the celebration of a version of radical autonomy, casts suspicion on any and all ties of reciprocal obligation and mutual interdependence. What counts in this scheme of things is only the individual and her choices. If choice is made absolute in this way, important and troubling questions that arise as one evaluates the distinction beteween individual right and social obligation are blanked out of existence. One simply gives everything, or nearly so, over to the individualist pole in advance. Ideally democratic individuality is "not

boundless subjectivist or self-seeking individualism,"
but the worry is that it has, over time, become such.[5]
The blessings of democratic life Tocqueville so bril-
liantly displayed, especially the spirit of equality,
including a certain informality and mixing of peoples of different stations, gives way and other more
fearful and self-enclosed, more suspicious and cynical, habits and dispositions rise to the fore.

In his recent book, *The True and Only Heaven*, the
historian and cultural critic Christopher Lasch tells
the tale this way. In the eighteenth century the
founders of modern liberalism embraced an argument that posited human wants and needs as ex-
pandable; indeed, nigh insatiable. It followed that
indefinite growth of the productive forces of economic life was needed in order to satisfy and
ongoingly fuel this restless cycle of needs-creation
and satiation. This ideology, called Progress, was
distinctive, Lasch claims, in exempting its world
from the judgement of time, leading to an unquali-
fied and altogether unwarranted optimism that a
way of life could persist untarnished, undamaged,
and without terrible pressure to its own, most cherished principles.

The joint property of various liberalisms and con-
servatisms, twentieth-century purveyors of Progress as an ideology celebrated a world of endless
growth, which meant in practice more and better
consumerism. Moving from a glorification of producer to consumer was key because the conclusion
was that underconsumption leads to declining in-

vestment. We want more and we want it now! All of life is invaded by the market and pervaded by market imagery. Perhaps we should not be too surprised that in America's inner cities young people rob, beat, even kill one another in order to steal expensive sneakers and gold chains, or that in America's suburbs young people whose families are well-off shun school and studies and community involvement in order to take part-time jobs to pay for consumer extras.

I take Lasch's argument to be similar to Pope John Paul II's criticism of "liberal capitalism" in "Sollicitudo Rei Socialis," his encyclical on social concerns. Rejecting the self-contained smugness of the ideology of Progress, John Paul scores a phenomenon he calls "superdevelopment, which consists in an excessive availability of every kind of material good for the benefit of certain social groups." Superdevelopment "makes people slaves of 'possession' and of immediate gratification, with no other horizon than the multiplication or continual replacement of the things already owned with others still better. This is the so-called civilization of 'consumption' or 'consumerism,' which involves so much 'throwing away' and 'waste.'"[6]

The "sad effects of this blind submission to pure consumerism," John Paul continues, is a combination of materialism and restless dissatisfaction as the "more one possesses the more one wants." Aspirations that cut deeper, that speak to human dignity within a world of others, are stifled. John Paul's name for this alternative aspiration is "solidarity," not "a feeling of vague compassion or shallow distress as the misfortunes of so many people" but, instead, a determination to "commit oneself to the common good; that is to say, to the good of all and of each individual because we are really responsible for all." Through solidarity, says John Paul, we *see* "the 'other' . . . not just as some kind of instrument . . . but as our 'neighbor,' a 'helper' . . . to be made a sharer on a par with ourselves in the banquet of life to which all are equally invited by God."[7]

To the extent that John Paul's words strike us as utopian or naive, to that extent we have lost civil society. Or so, at least, the sociologist Alan Wolfe concludes in *Whose Keeper? Social Science and Moral Obligation*. Wolfe updates Tocqueville, apprising us of how far we have come, or how rapidly we have travelled, down the road to more and more bad individualism, requiring more and more management, control, and concentration of political and economic power in order to keep us bounded in our little kingdoms of one. Wolfe suggests that for all our success in modern societies, especially in the United States, there is a sense, desperate in some cases, that all is not well, that something has gone terribly awry. We citizens of liberal democratic societies understand and cherish our freedom but we are, according to Wolfe, "confused when it comes to recognizing the social obligations that make . . . freedom possible in the first place."[8] This confusion permeates all levels, from the marketplace, to the home, to the academy.

The confusion has a lot to do with a new attitude toward rights that has taken hold in the United States during the past couple of decades. Americans have been speaking the language of rights for a long time. It is part of our heritage, as American as apple pie. Recall, if you will, the first noticeable mention of rights as the Bill of Rights got appended to, and became part of, the American Constitution. These rights revolve around civic freedoms — assembly, press, speech — and around what government cannot do to you, say, unreasonable search and seizure. Rights were designed primarily as immunities, as a way to protect us from overweening governmental power, not as entitlements. The rights-bearing individual was a civic creature, a community creature, a family man or woman located within the world of civil society I described above. But, as time passed, the rights-bearing individual came to stand alone: me and my rights. And rights got construed increasingly in individualistic terms as the civic dimensions of rights withered on the vine. What were previously seen simply as personal wants are now demanded as rights. These run the gamut from demands for sexual satisfaction, self-esteem, and uninhibited self-expression as "rights" to the notion that everyone, without exception, has a "right" to a vast array of consumer choices. As Mary Ann Glendon points out in *Rights Talk,* missing are dimensions of sociality and responsibility as rights and the rights-defined self stand alone.[9]

This dynamic helps us to make sense of the political fallout from "rights talk" that surely puts democracy

on trial. Let me elaborate by developing further one
of my earlier claims. We now witness a morally
exhausted left embracing rather than challenging
the logic of the market by endorsing the relentless
translation of *wants* into *rights*. Although the political left continues to argue for taming the market in
a strictly economic sense, it follows the market
model where social relations are concerned, seeing
in any restriction of individual "freedom" to live any
sort of "lifestyle," as we call it today, an unacceptable
diminution of rights and free expression. On the
other hand, many on the political right love the
untrammelled (or the less trammelled the better)
operations of the market in economic life but call for
a restoration of traditional morality, including strict
sexual and social scripts for men and women in
family and work life. Both rely either on the market
or the state to "organize their codes of moral obligation, but what they really need," Wolfe insists, "is
civil society — families, communities, friendship
networks, solidaristic workplace ties, voluntarism,
spontaneous groups and movements — not to re-
ject, but to complete the project of modernity."[10]

What is needed to speed this cherished end is a
return to a more thoroughly social understanding of
rights: rights are always transitive; they always involve us with others. Rights cannot stand alone.
Rights cannot come close to exhausting who and
what we are. Should we try to understand why we
stay up all night with a sick child, or take our neighbour a pot of soup when she comes home from the
hospital, or spend hours helping to provision the

victims of a natural disaster (like a flood or a hurricane) in and through "rights talk," we would seriously distort these socially responsible and compassionate activities. We know this in our bones. Yet each time we feel called upon to justify something politically, the tendency is to make our concerns far more individualistic and asocial than they, in fact, are, by reverting to the language of rights as a "first language" of liberal democracy.

None of the thinkers I have mentioned finds a solution to our Tocquevillian anxiety in a more powerful state, even if one includes the welfare state as we know it. The most highly developed welfare state in nineteenth-century Europe was Bismarck's "welfare-warfare" state, one in which social benefits were geared explicity to making the poor loyal dependents on the state. Social control was the aim; welfare the strategy. For most of us in the modern West the welfare state emerged out of a set of ethical concerns and passions that grew as civil society began to succumb to market forces. These concerns ushered in the conviction that the state was the "only agent capable of serving as a surrogate for the moral ties of civil society." But a half century of evidence is in and it is clear that the logic of state provision and the creation of classes of long-term dependents itself erodes further "the very social ties that make government possible in the first place."[11]

Let me be clear here. I am not so naive or foolish as to believe we can do without the state. The state, properly chastened, plays a vital role in a democratic society. Rather, I am worried about the *logic* of statism.

This logic is one that looks to the state first as the only entity capable of "solving a problem," or responding to a concern. But as the state expands its role, the capacities of local institutions are further diminished. That is one problem. Another is what might be called the *ideology* of statism, an ideology not so prevalent in North American democracy as it was in those civic republican polities imagined by Jean-Jacques Rousseau and implemented over time by civic actors, including the French revolutionaries.

The statist is one who wants to thin out the ties of civil society even further, who hopes to erode the force of the plural loyalties and diverse imperatives these give rise to and sustain. The statist citizen is represented as unhesitatingly loyal to the state and prepared to give primacy to it and its purposes. The statist identifies us primarily as creatures available for mobilization by a powerful centralized mechanism, rather than as family men and women, neighbours, members of a fraternal order or a feminist health cooperative, activists trying to save the African elephant from extinction, participants in a reading group, Baptists, Catholics, and so on. The statist wants us hemmed in and obliged in all sorts of mandated ways.

But the citizen of a democratic civil society understands that government cannot substitute for moral obligations — it can either deplete or nourish them. As our sense of particular, morally grounded responsibilities to an intergenerational web and a world of friends and neighbours falters, and the state moves in to treat the dislocations, it may temporarily solve delimited problems broadly defined but these very solutions, in time, serve to further thin out the skein of obligation. Eventually support for the state itself begins to plummet — people feel anomic and aggrieved, their resentments swell — and one sees the evidence in tax evasion, an upsurge in violence against persons and property, the breakup of social ties, including families, on an unprecedented scale, the rise of political cynicism, even something akin to despair.

A number of contemporary observers see such signs of civic and social trouble even in the long-established welfare democracies of Western Europe and Scandinavia. It is, alas, the by now familiar story: the loneliness of the aged; the apathy of the young; the withering away of churches and communal organizations; the disentangling of family ties and the rituals and rhythms of family life. I don't want to say that welfare provision directly caused any of this. I do want to suggest that a strong, bureaucratically top-heavy state that numbers among its tasks defining populations by their "needs" and targeting them for various reform efforts based on assumptions about such needs really cannot help moving in a "social engineering" direction that exists in tension with democratic freedom, civic sociality, and individual liberty.

Now it is no doubt the case that there is a distinction to be made between the dominant rhetoric of individualism and the culture of cynicism and how, in fact, we act as members of families, communities, churches, and neighbourhoods. Perhaps. But surely

it is true that our social practices are under extraor-
dinary pressure. This means democracy itself is
being squeezed. Fearful people want more law and
order and stiffer penalties for offenders. In America
they rush to arm themselves, believing safety is
more and more a matter of aggressive self-help.
Angry people want all the politicians kicked out, but
they believe new ones will be no better. Anxious
people fear that their neighbour's child may get
some unfair advantage over their own. Despairing
people destroy their own lives and the lives of those
around them. Muddled people flit wildly from one
thing to another, disorganized and unsure of who
they are and what they are to do. Careless people
ignore their children and then blast the teachers and
social workers who must tend to the mess they have
made, screaming that folks ought to "mind their
own business." Many human ills cannot be cured,
of course. All human lives are lived on the edge of
quiet desperation. We must all be rescued from time
to time from fear and sorrow. But I read the palpable
despair and cynicism and violence as dark signs of
the times, as warnings that democracy may not be
up to the task of satisfying yearnings it itself un-
leashes — yearnings for freedom, and fairness, and
equality.

Let us take a closer look. Counsels of despair are
of little help and rapidly descend into bathos and
even self-indulgence. One sign that democracy is on
trial is a falling away from the firm, buoyant conviction of democrats that a rights-based democratic
equality, guaranteed by the vote, would serve over

time as the sure and secure basis of a democratic culture. Political theorist George Kateb, for example, describes and celebrates "democratic individuality," reflected in and protected by "the electoral procedure, the set of rules" that embody "great value of equal respect for persons." Such rules, including the franchise as a right, radiate "a strong influence" that goes much beyond the formal prerogatives themselves, helping to instill a sense of dignity and permanently chastening political authority should it grow overweening.[12] Kateb does well to remind us of the distinction between destructive individualism and the ennobling strengths of the democratic tradition of respect for the human person, taken as a single, unique, and irreplaceable self.

But a striking feature of our epoch is that those very rights, the terms of democratic equality itself, have fallen into disrepute. Rather than serving as a frame within which democratic individuality can be shored up — in which a self made possible by the debates and dialogues a rule-governed democratic culture sustains — we hear ever more cynical appraisals of the rules, regulations, procedures, guarantees, and premises of constitutional democracy itself. For example, fuelled by claims that wildly exaggerate the ubiquity of violence perpetrated against women — for media hysteria knows no restraint in this matter — various proposals have been made that begin from the premise that burdensome democratic procedures, including the presumption of innocence, be seen for what they are: bourgeois hypocrisy, nothing more, nothing less. Rather than recognize in the presumption of innocence (i.e., the need for my accusers to bear the burden of proof), protection for myself or my loved ones should we ever be called before the bar of justice, we read articles challenging the whole idea of evidentiary requirements, central to the ideal of equal standing before the law.

This short temper with honouring the rights of the accused and meting out punishment appropriate to fit the concrete, particular crime that may have occurred is, for example, powerfully evident in a piece of legislation pending in the United States Senate. Called the Violence Against Women Act of 1993, the legislation incorporates "gender motivation" into a law that presumes to find in rape the paradigmatic, indeed normative, expression of male domination. Thus one moves away from the guiding presumptions of democratic jurisprudence, namely, that each case must be looked at individually: one must assess what happened to this victim, what got perpetrated by that offender. But the defenders of this new approach assume an undifferentiated class of victimizers (male) against an undifferentiated class of victims (female). This notion raises the spectre that the concrete facts in a case of sexual assault will be much less important in establishing guilt or innocence than some vague "animus based on a victim's gender." The motive police here rely on the platitudes of radical feminist ideology, a view of the moral and social world that, in the words of Catharine MacKinnon, "stresses the indistinguishability of prostitution, marriage, and sexual harassment." In this scheme of things sex is what men do *to* women. In a society characterized by what is routinely called the "systemic oppression of women," men simply *are* rapists, either actual or in situ. What is lost is the truth expressed by our new Supreme Court Justice, Ruth Bader Ginsburg, that "generalizations about the way women or men are ... cannot guide me reliably in making decisions about particular individuals." We find, then, at this very moment the rather distressing spectacle of an assault on civil liberties coupled with a perfervid ideology of victimization. Small wonder American politics so perplexes those who observe it.

Charles Taylor rightly notes the tremendous amount of activity discernible in American politics, an incessant hubbub, as a matter of fact, but he describes the American political scene as dismal, in part because American society has grown ever more fragmented. He writes: "A fragmented society is one whose members find it harder and harder to identify with their political society as a community. This lack of identification may reflect an atomistic outlook, in which people come to see society purely instrumentally. But it also helps to entrench atomism, because the absence of effective common action throws people back on themselves."[13] We are thrown back on ourselves into the ever-raging currents of consumer excess, or the cold comfort of ever more computerized and centralized bureaucracies.

I think of the words now used to characterize American politics: stalemate, gridlock, cynicism.

American politics is a miasma, so argue many of our experts and journalists, as well as our ordinary citizens. But this growing cynicism about politics promotes a spiral of delegitimation. How does a spiral of delegitimation get a society in its grip? Over a period of time what I called earlier a "culture of mistrust" grows, aided and abetted, by an ever more litigious society; by a determination to "get mine" no matter what may happen to the other guy; by salacious snooping into the private lives of public figures, which further fuels cynicism about how untrustworthy our leaders are even as we delight in their downfall.

It is quite a mess, but it isn't America's mess alone. Perhaps it is worth noting that the growth in American cynicism about democratic government shifts America toward, not away from, a more generalized norm. Most people in other societies are somewhat cynical about government, including citizens of the democracies of Western Europe. As James Q. Wilson points out, Americans "are less optimistic and less trusting than we once were. And rightly so," he goes on, "if Washington says that we should entrust it to educate our children, to protect our environment, and to regulate our economy, we would be foolish not to be cautious and skeptical."[14] The problem, according to Wilson, is that government has become less effective, not so much as a result of its size per se but because government since the 1960s has taken on more and more issues that it is simply ill-equipped to handle well — abortion and race relations, to name two of the most volatile. Too many such "wedge issues," as the pundits and strategists call them, were created, not by cynical demagogues, but by well-meaning federal judges presiding over courts who made decisions in the 1960s and 1970s on a whole range of cultural questions without due consideration of how public support for mandated outcomes might be generated.

Dealing with abortion, to take up but one example of a controversial ethical and cultural issue, is very different from building a great interstate highway system. All the cultural questions that now pit democratic citizens against one another — in addition to abortion I think of family values, drugs, and race relations — have been joined in ways that guarantee they will continue to divide us, in large part because of the means government used to put these issues on the table, often through judicial fiat. So it was in the deeply contentious *Roe v. Wade* case guaranteeing abortion on demand. This 1973 decision by the Supreme Court preempted a nationwide political debate that was raging in nearly every state at the time. Indeed, some sixteen states had already reformed their abortion statutes, making abortion more widely available. As well, as Michael Barone, a historian of this continuing saga has pointed out, "By the time the *Roe v. Wade* decision was issued, about 70% of the nation's population lived within 100 miles — an easy two hours' drive — of a state with a legalized abortion law. And just as the Supreme Court was speaking, legislatures in almost all of the states were going into session; many would probably have liberalized their abortion laws if the court had not acted."[15]

I offer this example not in order to take a stand on abortion but to take a stand against juridical moves that freeze out citizen dialogue. Juridical politics is black and white; it is adversarial; it is winner-take-all. The juridical model of politics, pushed by liberal activists originally, now embraced by their conservative counterparts, preempts democratic contestation and a politics of respect and melioration. When the Supreme Court threw all its weight to one side in a highly fraught situation in which people of goodwill differed, it aroused from the beginning strong and shocked opposition from those who despaired that their government, at its highest level, sanctioned what they took to be the destruction of human life at its most vulnerable stage. By guaranteeing that pro-abortion and anti-abortion forces need have no debate over time with one another, other than through judges, the court deepened a politics of resentment. There are, alas, many more examples of this sort.

But I fear I shall weary the reader should I tell further tales of our discontents. Let us look, instead, at a few proposed solutions and assess whether they promise democratic renewal or something else altogether. One panacea sought by some impatient with the compromises and mediations of democratic civil society, and frustrated whether by government inaction or too much action but of a sort they oppose, is a direct by contrast to a representative democratic system. Let the people speak! This populist theme is a recurring refrain in American political life. Historically populists often wanted government off their backs and power restored to their own communities. Currently populists feed on mistrust and anti-elitism — and anyone unlucky enough to hold a government office of any kind is subject to their ire.

In the American presidential elections of 1992, populist fervour gained surprising strength in the person, and candidacy, of the Texas millionaire Ross Perot. Perot is far less important than the phenomenon he helped to catalyze. Consider, briefly, one of his proposed cures for democratic ills, a cure that has been endorsed, to ends rather different from Perot's, by some commentators on the left, as well. Such populists, or strong democrats as they like to be called, would perfect democracy by eliminating barriers between the people's will and its forthright articulation. Pure democracy beckons, whirring and humming in the background of such visions, sometimes called "the electronic town hall."

It would work like this: American democracy is in trouble because the direct expression of the people's will is thwarted. But technology will come to our rescue through instant plebiscites via interactive television and telepolling. Should we include managed competition in a health-care proposal? Press the yes button or the no button. Should we bomb Baghdad because of yet another Saddam Hussein blunder or nefarious scheme? Press that button. What those who push such techno-solutions fail to appreciate is that plebiscitary majoritarianism is quite different from the dream of a democratic polity sustained by debate and judgement. Plebiscites have been used routinely to shore up anti-democratic, majoritarian movements and regimes — Argentinian Peronism comes to mind.

Even if one could devise a way to "sample" the political responses of the 120 million households in the United States, the plebiscite solution to democratic disillusionment must be criticized no matter who is championing its use. The distinction between a democratic and a plebiscitary system is no idle one. In a plebiscitary system the views of the majority can more easily swamp minority or unpopular views. Plebiscitism is compatible with authoritarian politics carried out under the guise of, or with the connivance of, majority opinion. That opinion can be registered ritualistically, so there is no need for debate with one's fellow citizens on substantive questions. All that is required is a calculus of opinion.

True democracy, Abraham Lincoln's "last, best hope on earth," is a rather different proposition. It requires, indeed its very lifeblood, is a mode of participation with one's fellow citizens animated by a sense of responsibility for one's society. The participation of plebiscitarianism is dramatically at odds with this democratic ideal. Watching television and pushing a button is a privatizing experience: it appeals to us as consumers, consumers of political decision-making in this instance, not as public citizens.

On the surface, being asked your opinion and being given a chance to register it instantly may seem democratic — one gets to make one's opinions known. But the "one" in this formulation is the private person enclosed within herself rather than the public citizen. A compilation of opinions does not make a civic culture; such a culture emerges only from a deliberative process. To see button-pressing or making a phone call as a meaningful act on a par with lobbying, meeting, writing letters to the editor, serving on the local school board, working for a candidate, helping to forge a coalition to promote a particular program or policy or to stop something bad from happening parallels a crude version of so-called "preference theory" in economics.

This theory holds that in a free-market society individual consumer choices result in the greatest benefit to society as a whole at the same time as they meet individual needs. The presumption behind this theory is that each and every one of us is a "preference maximizer." Aside from being a simplistic account of human motivation, preference theory lends itself to a blurring of important distinctions. According to preference maximizers, there is no such thing as a social good — there are only aggregates of private goods. Measuring our opinions through electronic town halls is a variant on this crude but common notion. It promises as a cure more of what ails us. Under the banner of more perfect democratic choice, we become complicit in eroding even further those elements of deliberation, reason, judgement, and shared goodwill that alone make genuine choice and democracy possible. We would turn our representatives into factotums, mouthpieces expressing our electronically generated will. This is a nightmare not a democratic dream.

Is there any way to break the spiral of mistrust and cynicism? Yes, but it will be difficult. Some, and I include myself in this number, embrace the idea of a new social covenant. What we have in mind goes like this: unless Americans, or the citizens of any faltering democracy, can once again be shown that they are all in it together; unless democratic citizens remember that being a citizen is a *civic* identity, not primarily a private sinecure; unless government can find a way to respond to people's deepest concerns, a new democratic social covenant has precious little chance of taking hold. But take hold it must if we are to stem the tide of divisive wedge issues that pit citizen against citizen in what social scientists call a zero-sum game: I win; you lose — that juridical model of politics I have already decried. The social covenant is not a dream of unanimity or harmony but the name given to a hope that we can draw on what we hold in common even as we disagree.

Let us imagine how a new social covenant might work in America's troubled cities and on her mean streets. A democratic social covenant would work to draw whites and blacks together around their shared concern for safe streets and neighbourhoods, in part by altering the terms of the public debate. The social covenanteer would tell liberals who espouse un-trammelled lifestyle options that they must forgo their disdain for the more stable values — especially those of family and religious faith — that most people cherish and the concerns to which those values give rise.

The interviews I have conducted with mothers and grandmothers who are active in anti-gang and anti-drug politics in their communities show clearly how much at odds their views are with a certain sort of liberal dogma that refuses to confront the realities of violence and even chaos in housing projects and dangerous streets. The problem, say the mothers and grandmothers, is too much freedom for armed persons, many of them teenagers, who prey on others and who are not taken off streets and out of the neighbourhoods they terrorize. They want more police patrols, more neighbourhood power, less freedom for armed teenagers to run amok, tougher penalties for crime.

The social covenanteer also recognizes that market strategies are ill-designed to speak directly to what concerns people the most in the worst of our inner-city neighbourhoods. He or she would tell gun advocates and civil libertarians that, yes, murderers do kill people, but they use guns to do it. Surely you would favour removing guns from the hands of dangerous people. Can you not assume that a fourteen-year-old drug-using dropout is dangerous, or potentially so? Would his freedom be unduly hampered if we made certain that he did not carry a gun into a school, a schoolyard, or a supermarket? The libertarian might respond that it is already against the law for minors to carry loaded firearms. But the tough-minded advocate of a social covenant would respond, "Yes, I know that. But the fact of the matter is that children in America's inner cities are armed and dangerous, primarily to one another. Surely we can begin the process of disarming!"

Take a second case. There are those prepared to

excuse violent outrages on the grounds that looting, pillaging, burning, and beating are expressions of "rage at social injustice." The social covenant message to them is to get a grip on reality and call things by their real names. When I read headlines in so-called progressive journals in the aftermath of the 1992 riots in Los Angeles proclaiming, "L.A. Uprising!" or "L.A. Rebellion," I felt real chagrin. A paternalistic, liberal racism that refuses to see all citizens as responsible remains racist. To excuse or even condone utterly random violence, marked not by marches and organizing into councils and issuing manifestos but by a looting frenzy tied to a brutal destruction of persons and property, is to perpetrate a sickly fascination with violence, as if shedding blood was inherently a political act, and a radical one at that. Such enchantment with violence ill serves not only its victims, primarily those in the neighbourhoods in which the riots occurred, but perpetuates what Hannah Arendt found to be one of the most pervasive and dangerous of all political ideas — and she indicted left and right alike for their enchantment with it at different times and in different places — the idea that something good comes out of something evil; that authentic politics flows from the barrel of a gun, or a knife blade, or a gasoline bomb.

Government can be effective in lowering the homicide and terror rate in inner-city neighbourhoods, and we do not need to abolish the Bill of Rights to accomplish these goals. But we do need, as a first step, to break through cynicism and anomie and to reverse the spiral of delegitimation. The democratic social covenant rests on the presumption that one's fellow citizens are people of goodwill who yearn for the opportunity to work together rather than to continue glaring at one another across racial, class, and ideological divides, assuming ill will on the part of others. To accomplish this reversal we must tend to the badly battered institutions of civil society I discussed at the outset.

An enormous task, yes, but worth our best efforts. As we enter the twenty-first century, we may learn, perhaps sooner than we would like, whether Lincoln's expression of the hope of American democracy was an epitaph or the harbinger of a brighter democratic future for America and hence for the world. For if the American republic falters it will be the crash heard round the world. Our many friends in other countries, especially in the young and fragile democracies, will tremble, falter, and perhaps fail without the ballast America uniquely provides given her power and her promise. That is the glorious burden of American democracy in the next century.

Once I was asked by Jamie Swift, a broadcaster who was putting together a radio series on "The U.S.A. Today" for CBC Radio's *Ideas*, "What does it mean to you to be an American?"

I faltered for a moment and mumbled that ubiquitous word "gosh" before I got my bearings and responded, "It means that one can share a dream of political possibility, which is to say, a dream of democracy. It means that one can make one's voice heard. It means both individual accomplishment as well as a sense of responsibility. It means sharing the possibility of a brotherhood and sisterhood that is perhaps fractious — as all brotherhoods and sisterhoods are — and yet united in some spirit that's a spirit more of good than ill will. It means that one is marked by history but not totally burdened with it and defined by it. It means that one can expect some basic sense of fair play . . . will be recalled and called upon. I think Americans are committed to a rough-and-ready sense of fair play, and a kind of *social* egalitarianism, if you will, an egalitarianism of manners. I think that's the best I can do."

I will try to do better in the next chapter in which I will hone in on a politics of displacement, a politics that dislodges the concerns of the citizen and public life in favour of politicizing all features of who and what we are. At stake is the delicate intertwining of public and private life characteristic of the democratic drama.

II

DEMOCRACY AND THE POLITICS OF DISPLACEMENT

HAVE WE DEMOCRATIC CITIZENS BECOME more fearful than hopeful? I suggested as much in my previous chapter in which I surveyed the deepening anxiety, anger, resentment, and apathy that put democracies on trial, and expressed my disagreement with a few ostensibly populist remedies to this condition. Let me remind you of a few of these fears — fear that the next generation's way of life will not, in fact, be better than that of previous generations; fear that our position in the world will falter; fear that communities will continue to disintegrate; fear that families will more and more collapse; fear that the centre simply will not hold. Fearful, we retreat or we participate in a politics of resentment in which we must find somebody or some group to blame for all our ills — foreigners without, enemies within. If the great Roman republican citizen Cicero lamented that "we have lost the *res publica*," I bemoaned the loss of something similar, the public citizen, and I embraced, as an alternative, a new social covenant in which we reach out once more to our fellow citizens from a stance of goodwill rather than ill humour and defuse our discontents in order that we might forge working alliances across various groups. Then and only then, I suggested, can we reclaim the great name — citizen — once again. For the citizen is the name we give to our public identities and actions in a democratic society.

But wait, some among you may proclaim, do we not see more and more activity, more and more public hustle and bustle as people take to the streets and the airwaves demanding recognition for who and what they are? Is there not a great deal of what you described as active participation in your previous chapter — lobbying, meeting, marching, debating? Is this not citizenship of the robust sort?

I must demur and hope that I will be successful, in what follows, in explaining the distinction to be marked between what I tag a *politics of displacement* by contrast to authentic democratic possibilities. Roughly put, a politics of displacement involves two trajectories. In the first, everything private — from sexual practices to anger at one's parents to insufficient self-assertiveness — becomes grist for the public mill. In the second, everything public — from the grounds on which politicians are judged to health policies to gun regulations — is itself privatized, the playing out of a psychodrama on a grand scale.

This merging of the public and private is anathema to democratic thinking, which holds that the distinction between public and private identities, commitments, and activities is of vital importance.

Historically it has been the anti-democrats who have insisted that political life must be cut from one piece of cloth — they have demanded overweening and unified loyalty to the city unclouded by other passions, loyalties, and interests. Something similar is going on as politics gets displaced in the ways I will unpack, beginning with a reminder of what we democrats are talking about when we evoke the terms *public* and *private*.

Public and private are terms of ordinary discourse. Public and private are always defined and understood in relationship to each other. One version of private means "not open to the public," and public, by contrast, is that "of or pertaining to the whole, done or made in behalf of the community as a whole." In part these contrasts derive from the Latin origins of *public*, *pubes*, the age of maturity when signs of puberty begin to appear: then and only then does the child enter, or become qualified for, public things. Similarly *publicus* is that which belongs to, or pertains to, "the public," the people. But there is another meaning: public as open to scrutiny; private as that not subjected to the persistent gaze of publicity. Here we glimpse matters not wholly revealed. This barrier to full revelation is necessary, or so defenders of constitutional democracy have long insisted, in order to preserve the possibility of different sorts of relationships — both the mother *and* the citizen, the friend *and* the official, and so on.

Minimally a *political* perspective requires that that activity we call "politics" be differentiated from other

activities and relationships. If all conceptual boundaries are blurred and all distinctions between public
and private are eliminated, no politics can exist by
definition. By politics I here refer to that which is,
in principle, held in common and that which is, in
principle, open to public scrutiny and judgement.
If I am correct and a politics of displacement is a
growing phenomenon, operating on the level of
elite opinion and popular culture alike, especially
in the United States, it bears deep implications for
how we will think about and do politics in the years
ahead.

A politics of displacement is a dynamic that con-
nects and interweaves public and private imperatives in a way that is dangerous to the integrity
of both. It is more likely to occur when certain conditions prevail. First, established public and private,
secular and religious, institutions and rules are in
flux and people have a sense that the centre will not
hold. Second, there are no clearly established public
institutions to focus dissent and concern in an ordered way. Third, and finally, private values, exigencies, and identities come to take precedence over
public involvement as a citizen.[16]

This is a world of triumphalist "I's," "a population of monads . . . simple, irreducible entities, each
defined by a unique point of view," in the words of
political theorist Sheldon Wolin.[17] To the extent there
is a "we" in this world of "I's," it is that of the discrete
group with which one identifies. For example, in
current debates over multiculturalism some argue
that, if one is an African-American, one must "think

black" and identify exclusively with one's racial group or designation. For persons thus identified the category of "citizen" is a matter of indifference at best; contempt at worst. More and more we see ourselves in exclusive terms along racial or gender or sexual preference lines. If this is who I am, why should I care about the citizen? That is for dupes who actually believed their high school civics class.

To the extent that a politics of displacement pertains, all is defined as "political" and watered down to the lowest common denominator. Thus, as I indicated in the first chapter, everything I "want" gets defined politically as a "right." This notion means my desire, now a right, to have easy access to a pornography channel on cable television is conflated to my right to be safe from arbitrary search and seizure. Authentic civil rights get trivialized in this process. Political ideals and private desires are blurred or collapsed. By extension, of course, there is no such thing as an authentically private sphere. Intimate life is pervaded with politics; private identity becomes a recommendation for, or authentication of, one's political stance. It follows that my rage quotient goes through the roof in political contestation because to argue against my public proclamations is, at one and the same time, to unhinge my private identity. This type of thinking is muddled, of course, but increasingly that is where we are at — to our own peril and that of our civic descendants.

Take, for example, the 1970s feminist slogan: the personal is political. On the one hand, this idea was an exciting and liberating move, compelling us to

attend to the undeniable fact that certain political
interests were often hidden behind a gloss of pro-
fessed concern for the sanctity of the private realm.
Feminists argued that political and ethical values
were often trivialized by being privatized. A whole
range of questions having to do with women, children, and families got sealed off as inappropriate to
political discussion and debate. Children's health,
for example, was the private concern of parents,
especially mothers, alone. But what if there is asbestos in the insulation of the local school building and
it is well-known that asbestos causes health problems? Surely, here, the threat to health is a public
one, involving all children — hence all families —
who attend or send their children to that school. To
politicize and to challenge the notion of separate
spheres — the male public world, the female private
world — in this way was a vital and important move.
Feminists committed to ideals of civility and civic
culture recognized that there were many ways to
carve up the universe of debate in social and political life. Well and good.

But there were problems from the beginning em-
bedded in the assertion that the personal is political
tout court. In its give-no-quarter form in radical feminist argumentation, any distinction between the
personal and political was disdained. Note that the
claim was not that the personal and political are
interrelated in important and fascinating ways previously hidden by sexist ideology and practice, nor
that the personal and political may be analogous to
each other along certain axes of power and privilege,

but that the personal *is* political. What got asserted was an identity, a collapse of one into the other. Nothing personal was exempt from political definition, direction, and manipulation — neither sexual intimacy, nor love, nor parenting. A total collapse of public and private as central categories of an enduring democratic drama followed. The private sphere fell under a thoroughgoing politicized definition. Everything, it seemed, was grist for a voracious public mill, nothing was exempt, there was nowhere to hide, and things got nasty fast. Women who continued to marry and to bear children became the target of all sorts of polemical assaults, for they were "collabos," women who collaborated with the male "enemy," women who had been turned into "mutilated, muted, moronized . . . docile tokens mouthing male texts," not a generous image to say the least, but one made possible by defining male-female relationships as *essentially* those of a victim to a victimizer.

But the big problem is not one of rhetorical excess, unpleasant as it was for those women getting called "fembots." No, the most serious dilemma — one that puts democracy ongoingly on trial — is simply this: if there are no distinctions between public and private, personal and political, it follows that no differentiated activity or set of institutions that are genuinely political, that are the purview of citizens and the bases of order, legitimacy, and purpose in a democratic community, exist. What does exist within the radical feminist script is pervasive force, coercion, and manipulation: power of the crassest sort suffusing the entire social landscape, from its

lowest to its loftiest points. If you live in a world of
pervasive fear and anxiety, a world this sort of rhetoric helps to construct, you become ripe — or so the
story of Western political thought warns us — for
anti-democratic solutions. If the problem is totalistic, so must the solution be. This notion goes against
the grain of the democratic temperament and democratic possibility that is always aware that no single
perspective, no single political platform or slogan,
can speak the whole truth about our situation.

There are few alternatives in such a world: one is
either victim or victimizer; oppressor or oppressed;
triumphant or abject. Politics as a differentiated
sphere of human activity disappears in this yearning for a totalistic solution to all human woes, a
thoroughgoing fusion of all principles. The possibility that certain vital relationships are possible *only*
because they are enacted against a backdrop that
thrusts some activities into the full glare of public
scrutiny and preserves others against scrutiny,
against snooping by roaming nosey parkers, as my
British friends call them, is simply forsworn.

Do I exaggerate? Perhaps. But let us take a closer
look. I hope to convince you that my concerns and
criticisms are warranted from a democratic point of
view. We have long been familiar with the terrible
invasion of private life and speech characteristic of
twentieth-century totalitarian societies. People in
such situations learn to censor themselves or, growing careless, may find that conversation around a
kitchen table, or in the bedroom with one's spouse,

becomes the public property of the police or, worse, of the entire society.

The Czech novelist Milan Kundera tells a chilling tale. In a 1984 interview with Philip Roth, Kundera notes a "magic border" between "intimate life and public life . . . that can't be crossed with impunity." For any "man who was the same in both public and intimate life would be a monster. He would be without spontaneity in his private life and without responsibility in his public life. For example, privately to you I can say of a friend who's done something stupid, that he's an idiot, that his ears ought to be cut off, that he should be hung upside down and a mouse stuffed in his mouth. But if the same statement were broadcast over the radio spoken in a serious tone — and we all prefer to make such jokes in a serious tone — it would be indefensible."[18]

Kundera goes on to recall the tragedy of a friend, a writer named Jan Prochazka, whose intimate "kitchen table" talks were recorded by the state police in pre-1989 Czechoslovakia and assembled into a "program" broadcast on state radio. Kundera writes of Prochazka: "He finds himself in a state of complete humiliation: the secret eye observes him even when he kisses his wife in the bedroom or stands in front of the toilet bowl. Such a man can only die." Prochazka did, by his own hand. According to Kundera, *intimate life,* a creation of European civilization "during the last 400 years," understood as "one's personal secret, as something valuable, inviolable, the basis of one's originality," is now in jeopardy everywhere, not just in statist societies with a secret police apparatus.

Are his fears well placed? Consider two examples drawn from contemporary American society, both flowing from a collapse of the personal into the political, both, therefore, exemplifying a politics of displacement. Of course, there are no precise parallels in a democratic society to the terror Kundera so poignantly describes. But we have our own "soft" versions of an utter disregard for public and private distinctions.

For my first example, let me zero in on an important concern — battered women — and take up various solutions to the problem proposed by some analysts and activists, solutions that display and deepen a politics of displacement; hence, an erosion of a public-private distinction. The first assertion usually made, and it is one all fair-minded persons will surely endorse, is to insist that domestic violence isn't just a private affair. But if you are working from a perspective that erodes any distinction between public and private, if you find this distinction nothing more than false "bourgeois hypocrisy," your proposed solutions start to take on many features of anti-democratic totalism.

The standard totalist case works like this: we must, as part of an interim strategy, expand the arrest powers of the police and promote the jurisprudential conviction that women are a special legal category requiring unique protection.[19] Precious little attention gets paid to the fact that enhancing police prerogatives to intervene may itself lead to abuse of society's least powerful persons — poor blacks, Hispanics, and so on, should they be deemed the most menacing members of a generic male threat. When this potential danger is acknowledged, it is usually seen as a chance worth taking. Mandated counselling, even behavioural conditioning of violent or "potentially" violent men, coupled with compulsory punishment and no appeal, are common as part of the panoply of interim proposals demanded; refusing to think about potential abuses inherent in extending the therapeutic powers of the state as part of its policing function is common.

While interim programs rely heavily on the state's policing powers (which, in other contexts, get trounced as part of the patriarchal order), the *solution* to the problem of ending violence once and for all requires a "total restructuring of society that is feminist, antiracist, and socialist," in the words of one advocate. But it is unclear whether such a society would be democratic or whether, indeed, there would be any politics worthy of the name at all. Remember the Marxist dream that one glorious day politics will come to an end, absorbed into administration in the future classless society. Presumably in this feminist version some sort of powerful state must be on hand to plan everything and to redistribute resources — given the commitment to socialism — but this is not spelled out.

Most important, in this new society imagined by Susan Schecter, a radical activist and writer, "family life would be open for *community scrutiny* because the family would be part of and accountable to the community. Community-based institutions could hear complaints and dispense justice, and community networks could hold individuals accountable for their behaviour and offer protection to women. If a *false separation* did not exist between the family and the community, women might lose their sense of isolation and gain a sense of entitlement to a violence-free life."[20] But what about the enormous, potential violence of the all-powerful community institutions and the state here envisaged? The author of this plan for eviscerating any public-private distinction goes no further in specifying how this robust communitarian world — a future perfect *Gemeinschaft* — is to be generated out of what she portrays as our current battlefield.

Because the advocate here cited blithely assumes that "total restructuring" will produce a moral consensus, all dissidents having been banished, silenced, punished, or reeducated, she skirts problems of coercion and control otherwise implicit in the scheme for hearing complaints and dispensing justice with no provisions for the accused having a defender and his accusers being cross-examined, and certainly no presumption of innocence until proven guilty. With every aspect of life opened up for inspection and, in her words, *scrutiny*, she prescribes a world democrats must find singularly unattractive, indeed, repellent.

Even in old-fashioned traditional communities of the sort I grew up in rural Colorado, a village of 185 human souls, there was room for backsliders, town drunks — we had ours, by the name of Pete Morton, may he rest in peace, loners, dreamers, and harmless eccentrics. Why do these prophets of totally restructured worlds "beyond compromise" not tell us what will happen to such folks in their brave new societies? Not every social misfit is a violent abuser. In the society of scrutiny, total accountability, and instant justice, the social space for difference, dissent, refusal, and indifference is squeezed out. This is where matters stand unless or until those feminists who share this theoretical orientation tell us how the future community of scrutiny will preserve any freedom worthy of the name.

I doubt, in fact, whether those making such proposals have really considered the implications of their arguments for democratic civil life. For example, contained within the paean to intrusive communities in a reconstructed future noted above is the unequivocal claim that "who women choose as emotional and sexual partners cannot be open for public scrutiny" — an embrace of the public-private distinction and the possibility for concealment wholly at odds with the plans for a society in which "family life will be open to community scrutiny."[21]

There seem to be a few loose threads dangling here. A more democratic way of tending to these matters is, in fact, to give wide berth to individuals to order their private lives as they see fit. Where the public begins to take a legitimate interest occurs when physical harm, persistent, not haphazard, a pattern, not an accident, occurs as one family member is beaten or bruised or injured by another. No democratic society can permit this assault on the dignity and standing of another to persist. We have devised ways — imperfect, to be sure — to deal with it that preserve our simultaneous commitment to protection for those who are being harmed and due process for those being accused. In part through the efforts of feminist organizers, the problem of battered women is now widely accepted as a public, not merely a private, concern. But this is quite different from arguing that everything that goes on inside a family is subject to public scrutiny.

Such a conjecture leads to another related concern — the notion that women are society's prototypical victims. There are, of course, real victims in the world and among their numbers are all too many women — assaulted, degraded, denied dignity. But an ideology of victimhood diverts attention from concrete and specific instances of female victimization in favour of pushing a relentless worldview structured around the victim/victimizer dichotomy. The aim is to promote what can only be called moral panic as women are routinely portrayed as deformed and mutilated, helpless and demeaned.

Note that the language of victimization describes women in passive terms. By losing all of the complexities of real victimization, women are recast as helpless prey for male lust. All women — all — are assaulted, although some may not yet recognize this; all are harmed, one way or another. Victimization ideology fuels female fear and, paradoxically, disempowers women rather than enabling them to see themselves as citizens with both rights and re-sponsibilities.

Several years ago I researched the question of women as crime victims. I learned that, on the best available evidence, the assertion that women are the *principal* victims of violent crime is false. As well, on the best available evidence, violence against women is *not*, as movement ideologues proclaim, on a precipitous upsurge as compared with other crimes. Yet popular perception, fuelled by victimization doctrine, holds otherwise. As a result, women more and more *think* of themselves as likely crime victims — they have assumed a victim ideology startlingly out of proportion to the actual threat. The perception of "women as victims" goes beyond a deeply rooted belief that violence against women is skyrocketing: it holds that women are special targets of crime in general and violent crime in particular. Yet the figures on this score have been remarkably consistent over the past decade: most perpetrators of violent crimes are males; most victims of violent crime are males similar in age and race to the perpetrators. Consistently the most victimized group is young men.

Fear-of-crime syndrome has a debilitating effect on female behaviour, for one internalizes a distorted perception of oneself. For example, habitual television viewers believe they have a fifty-fifty chance each week of being victims of a violent crime — an absurd figure. In 1991 in America half of the 250 made-for-television movies depicted women undergoing abuse of one kind or another. Often such

programs are given a feminist gloss. In fact, they ill
serve women, any feminism worthy of the name, or
the possibility of democratic citizenship by portray-
ing women as in peril in the home, the workplace,
the factory, and the street. Women are either
trembling wrecks or fierce avengers with scant regard for what is usually called "due process."

✳ My second example of a politics of displacement
is drawn from the intense arena of so-called "identity politics," of which I will speak in detail in a
subsequent chapter on democratic education and
the politics of difference. Remember that a central
characteristic of a politics of displacement is that
private identity takes precedence over public ends
or purposes; indeed, one's private identity becomes
who and what one is *in* public and what public life
is about is confirming that identity. The citizen gives
way before the aggrieved member of a self-defined
group. Because the group is aggrieved — the word
of choice in most polemics is "enraged" — the civility inherent in those rule-governed activities that
allow a pluralist society to persist falters. This assault on civility flows from an embrace of what
might be called a politicized ontology, that is to say,
persons are more and more judged not by what they
do or say but by what they *are*. What you are is what
your racial or sexual identity dictates. One's identity
becomes the sole and only ground of politics, the
sole and only determinant of political good and evil.
Those who disagree with my "politics," then, are the
enemies of my identity.

For my example of identity politics I turn to the

gay liberation movement. Gay liberation stands in contrast to an equal rights agenda that emphasizes an inclusive strategy on the part of gays to attain full citizenship, including a demand for dignity and recognition. I have participated in this latter effort myself, chairing a task force that established a Committee on the Status of Lesbians and Gays for the American Political Science Association. Our statement of principles emphasized collegiality and dignity and an insistence that persons hired to join one's academic department should be invited to full participation in the life of that department without regard to sexual orientation. Bad behaviour is bad behaviour, whether committed by a homosexual or a heterosexual, and only behaviour, not identity, should be criticized.

But mark this: from the beginning of the movement for gay liberation there was tension in the claim that gays, labelled an "oppressed class" by radical theorists, were forced to call upon the very society oppressing them not only to protect their rights, but to legitimate what got called a "homosexual ethos" or a "gay lifestyle." The argument that gays are oppressed, then, resulted in several very different sorts of claims: either that society has no business scrutinizing the private sexual preferences of anybody, including gays; or, that government *must* intrude in the area of private identity because gays, too, require a unique sort of public protection and "validation," in today's tedious lexicon.[22] A politics of democratic civility and equity holds that gays or any other group of citizens have a right, as

individuals, to be protected from intrusion or harassment, as well as a right to be free from discrim-
ination in employment, housing, and other areas.
This I take as a given where a public-private distinction of a certain sort is cherished and upheld. This
distinction is an ongoing imperative in a democratic constitutional system which, if ignored or
violated, represents more than an illegality: it is an
assault on the constitutive political ethic of a democratic society.

But no one has a *civil* right, whether as a gay, a
devotee of an exotic religion, or a political dissident,
to public sanction of his activities, values, beliefs, or
habits. To be publicly legitimated, or "validated" in
one's activities, beliefs, or habits may be a political
aim — indeed, it is the overriding aim of a politics
of displacement — but it is scarcely a civil right.
Paradoxically, in a quest to attain sanction for the *full*
range of who one is, whether as a devotee of sado-
masochistic enactments, or a cross-dresser, or whatever, the variations are nigh endless, one puts one's
life on full display, one opens oneself up fully to
publicity in ways others are bound to find quite
uncivil, in part because a certain barrier — the political philosopher, Hannah Arendt, would call it the
boundary of shame — is blatantly breached.

Now I readily admit that it is very difficult to
mount a defence of the necessity for shame in
today's world. But if, as I have argued, and many of
my betters before me, notably Tocqueville, have
insisted, democracy is about constitutions and rules
and public accountability and deliberation, yes, but

also about everyday life, about habits and dispositions, then it makes some sense to think about
shame and shamelessness. Shame or its felt experience as it surrounds our body's functions, passions,
and desires requires symbolic forms, veils of civility
that conceal some activities and aspects of ourselves
even as we boldly and routinely display and reveal
other sides of ourselves when we take part in public
activities in the light of day for all to see. When one
opens one's body up to publicity, and when one's
intimate life is put on display, one not only invites,
one actively seeks the exploitation of one's own body
to a variety of ends not fully under one's own control.
For one has withdrawn the body's intimacy from
interpersonal relations and exposed it to an un-
known audience who will make of it what they will.
Thus one may become an occasion for scandal or
abuse or even violence toward others through one's
own relentless self-exposure. Flaunting one's most
intimate self, making a public thing of oneself, is
central to a politics of displacement; arguing for a
position, winning approval, or inviting dissent as a
citizen is something quite different.

Shame is central to safeguarding the freedom of
the body. Small wonder, then, that so many philosophers and theologians and political theorists find
in shame a vital and powerful feature of our human
condition that we would overturn at our peril. This
is not to embrace duplicity and disguise; rather, it
means holding on to the concealment necessary to a
rich personal life and to human dignity in order that
one might know and thus work to attain that which

is self-revelatory, public, central to human solidarity and fellowship, what is in common.

✳ In Western democracies governed by notions of rights and the rule of law, the politically and culturally different have traditionally embraced certain principles of civility as their best and most enduring guarantee that government will not try to coerce them to concur with, or conform to, the majority. If I go about my business in a way respectful of the fact that you, too, must go about your business, we need not share nor even understand each other's beliefs, rituals, and values completely. But we do understand that we share a civil world; that we are, for better or for worse, "in it together."

Militant gay liberationists, however, in contrast to gay civil rights advocates, seek government protection and approval of their private identities and behaviour. The end point of these claims against society requires public remedies, for example, wrenching disclosures and invasions of the privacy of others called "outings," — the name given to a procedure whereby gays who prefer not to go public with their sexual orientation are forced "into the open" by other gays who publish their names in newspapers, post their pictures on telephone posts, broadcast their names in rallies, and the like. Such an activity might well have the practical result of strengthening the ethos of a society of scrutiny: nothing is exempt, if not from one's "enemies," then, ironically, even tragically, from one's ostensible friends and allies. As a result, the demand for public validation of sexual preferences, by ignoring the distinction between the personal and the political, threatens to erode authentic civil rights.

What follows from this version of "the personal is political" is the presumption that being gay is in itself a political act, condition, statement, or claim. For those pushing a strong version of identity politics, any politics that doesn't revolve around their identities is of no interest to them. There is no broader identification with a common good beyond that of the group of which one is a member. Hence, the argument, made in America's Vietnam era by an identity politics activist, that gays "do not get validated by our participation in anti-war marches" becomes understandable, because in anti-war marches one made common cause with other citizens who found the war abhorrent. If politics is reducible to the "eruption of radical feelings," something as ordinary as protest against an unjust war lacks revolutionary panache.[23] Personal authenticity becomes the test of political credibility. One can cure one's personal ills only through political rebellion based on sexual identity. The sorts of demands that issue from such a politics of displacement go far beyond a quest for civic freedom and for what Greek democrats called *isonomia*, equality: nothing less than personal happiness and sexual gratification are claimed as a *political* right.

The demand upon activists themselves is extreme, for every aspect of their lives must serve as a political statement. There is no surcease; no possibility to say, "To hell with it, I'm going fishing. I'll be a citizen again in two weeks." There is good reason for the democrat to be queasy about all this resolute militancy. Identity absolutism lends itself to expressivist politics, the celebration of feelings or private authenticity as an alternative to public reason and political judgement. Where is the check on over-personalization? There is none. It is perhaps useful at this juncture to remind those embracing a world without a public-private distinction that the world is much wider, deeper, and more mysterious than a wholesale mapping of the subjective self onto that world suggests. It is a world with saving graces, or hopefully so, a world of veils as well as mirrors, a world filled with all sorts of people with ingrained predispositions that may not, in fact, be trimmed precisely to fit the pattern we dictate.

When utopians of any stripe assault the idea of political standing in and through an ideal of the citizen, they promote the diminution of democratic politics in favour of a fantasy of a wholly transparent community in which all that divides us has been eliminated, or one in which our divisions are "beyond compromise." At the height of the 1960s Civil Rights Movement in America, Martin Luther King declared that he and his fellow citizen protestors were not asking their opponents to love them; rather, "We're just asking you to get off our backs."

King's dream of a new democratic community, a new social covenant, drew upon very old democratic ideas forged on the anvil of his rock-bottom Christian faith. In the world of practical politics King endorsed, pragmatic yet idealistic, blacks and whites, men and women, the poor and the privileged could come together around a set of concrete concerns. Temporary alliances get formed. On one issue, most of the blacks, say, may be on one side — although the assumption is never that things will automatically divide by racial or any other identity. There is, there must be, a way for people who differ in important, not trivial respects, to come together to do practical politics. The distinction between public and private life here marked grows from a recognition that while people's self-interests or personal travail may lead them to public action, the best principles of action in public are not reducible to a merely private matter. In public we learn to work with people with whom we disagree sharply and with whom we would not care to live in a situation of intimacy. But we can be citizens together; we can come to know a good in common we cannot know alone.

When I was in graduate school in the late 1960s, it was in vogue to mock the warnings of Isaiah Berlin about the dangers inherent in many visions of "positive liberty," turning as they did on naive views of a perfectible human nature and a utopian projection of a political solution to every human frailty and ill. Those who embraced "positive liberty" believed politics, or the only politics worthy of the name, must engage in massive rearrangement of human societies in order to attain an abstract goal of justice, say, or happiness on earth. Berlin was accused of being a "liberal sellout," a fainthearted compromiser, because he found such pictures of a future perfect reality implausible. But compromise, not as a mediocre way to do politics, but as the *only* way to do democratic politics, is itself an adventure. It lacks the panache of revolutionary violence. It might not stir the blood in the way a "non-negotiable demand" does. But it presages a livable future.

I am here reminded of a conversation I had in Prague in the summer of 1990 with a former dissident who found himself elected to Parliament in the aftermath of the remarkable events of November 1989. He said to me, "We've got a real problem here, because we are not habituated to democracy. We have had democratic moments in our past, but we don't have well-formed democratic dispositions. It will be difficult to build these up. It will take time. After all," he continued, "the democratic ideal is a very difficult ideal."

I asked him what he meant by that and he responded, "It is a difficult ideal, especially for people who have lived in a system of totalistic politics, because it embeds at its heart the ideal of compromise. In a democracy, compromise is not a terrible thing. It is necessary. It lies at the heart of things because you have to accept that people are going to have different views, especially on the most volatile matters and the most important issues."

His words struck me then and do so now because we, in our own democracies, are not doing very well at nurturing those democratic dispositions that encourage people to accept that they can't always get everything they want and that, moreover, it is possible that some of what they seek in politics is not, in fact, to be found there.

In any democratic polity there are choices to be made that involve both gains and losses. Berlin reminds us that a "sharp division between public and private life, or politics and morality, never works well. Too many territories have been claimed by both." But to collapse public and private altogether is an even worse prospect for, according to Berlin, "the best that one can do is to try to promote some kind of equilibrium, necessarily unstable, between the different operations of different groups of human beings — at the very least to prevent them from attempting to exterminate one another and, so far as possible, to prevent them from hurting each other — and to promote the maximum practicable degree of sympathy and understanding, never likely to be complete between them."[24] This is a plea for practical politics within a democratic polity characterized by civility and open to the possibility of achieving working majorities, provisional commonalities, and no doubt ephemeral moments of civic virtue.

A richly complex private sphere requires freedom from an all-encompassing public imperative in order to survive. But in order for it to flourish the public world itself must nurture and sustain a set of ethical imperatives, including a commitment to preserve, protect, and defend human beings in their capacities as private individuals and public citizens engaged in the practical activity of democratic life. This ideal keeps alive a fruitful if, at times, frustrating tension between diverse spheres and competing ideals and purposes. There is always a danger that a too strong and overweening polity will swamp the individual, as well as a peril that life in a polity confronted with a continuing crisis, a politics of displacement, may decivilize both those who oppose it and those who promote it.

III

DEMOCRACY AND THE POLITICS OF DIFFERENCE

THE QUESTION OF THE ONE AND THE MANY, of unity and diversity, has been posed from the beginning of political thought in the West. The American Founders were well aware of the vexations attendant upon the creation of a new political body. They worked with, and against, a stock of metaphors that had previously served as the symbolic vehicles of political incorporation. As men of the Enlightenment, they rejected images of the body politic that had dominated medieval and early modern political thinking. For a Jefferson or a Madison such tropes as "the King's two bodies" or John of Salisbury's twelfth-century rendering, in his *Polycraticus,* of a body politic with the Prince as the head and animating force of other members were too literalist, too strongly corporatist, and too specifically Christian to serve the *novus ordo saeclorum.* But they were nevertheless haunted by Hebrew and Christian metaphors of a covenanted polity: the body is one but has many members. There is, there can be, unity with diversity.

Indeed, one could even go so far as to insist that

it is incorporation within a single body that makes
meaningful diversity possible. Our differences must
be recognized if they are to exist substantively at all.
As Charles Taylor writes: "[M]y discovering my own
identity doesn't mean that I work it out in isolation,
but that I negotiate it through dialogue, partly overt,
partly internal, with others. . . . My own identity cru-
cially depends on my dialogical relations with others."[25] What this means is that we cannot be different
all by ourselves. A political body that simulta-
neously brings people together, creating a "we," but
enables these same persons to separate themselves
and to recognize one another in and through their
differences as well as in what they share in common — that was the great challenge of the Founding
Fathers. It remains the great challenge.

I indicated in the previous chapter that one version
of our current discontents — the politics of displacement — tries to solve this problem by smashing it to
bits. Rather than negotiating the complexity of public
and private identities, the citizen, whether male or
female, whether heterosexual or homosexual, black
or white, any such distinction — between citizen and
whatever else I may be — is disdained and displaced.
One seeks full public recognition as an African-
American or a person with a handicap or a particular
sexual orientation and that exhausts one's public concerns. Marks of difference, once they gain public
recognition, acceptance, legitimation, or even pre-
ferred status and treatment, are triumphant. The
public world is a world of many "I's" who form a
"we" only with others exactly like themselves. No

recognition of commonality is forthcoming. We are stuck in what the philosopher calls a world of "incommensurability," a world in which we quite literally cannot understand one another.

Democrats historically would have found this peculiar at best; anathema at worst. Democrats today are troubled by such developments. We recognize in the rush for recognition of difference a powerful, and legitimate, modern concern. Some forms of equal recognition are surely not only possible in a democracy but form its very lifeblood. The question is — what sort of recognition? Recognition of what? For what? To claim, "I am different, you must recognize me and honour my difference," tells me nothing, nothing at all. Should I honour someone, recognize her, simply because she is female or proclaims a particular version of her sexual identity? This makes little sense. I may disagree profoundly with her about everything I find important — from what American policy ought to be in the war in the Balkans, to what needs to be done to stem the tide of deterioration and despair in America's inner cities, to whether violence on television is a serious concern or just an easy target for riled and worried parents and educators.

My recognition of her difference — by which I mean my preparedness to engage her as an interlocutor, *given* our differences on the things that count politically, namely, equality, justice, freedom, fairness, authority, power, and so on — turns on the fact that I share something with her — she is in the world with me; she, too, is a citizen. We both, hopefully, operate from a stance of goodwill and an acceptance of the backdrop of democratic constitutional guarantees and democratic habits and dispositions, including a commitment to rough-and-ready parity, an energetic desire to forge at least provisional agreements on highly controversial issues and, if we cannot, to remain committed nonetheless to the centrality of dialogue and debate to our shared way of life. If I am her enemy — because I am white or heterosexual or a mother or an academic at an elite institution — her only desire can be to silence me, to reproach me, or to wipe me out. One makes war with enemies; one does politics — democratic politics — with opponents.

I will turn to how we come to know something "in common," to accept that we share a heritage although we share it imperfectly and unevenly, in a moment. But, first, let me say more about the current politics of difference. At one point, not all that long ago, it was the liberal position that an emphasis on the ways people differed sanctioned inequality. No, argued liberal thinkers, it is our "sameness" that alone secures an egalitarian, democratic regime. After all, was it not hierarchical, inegalitarian, conservative thinkers who insisted that natural differences would also translate into social and political inequalities? American society is, perhaps, unique among nations in building in from the first a strong presumption for equality as one of the touchstones of its national identity and political culture: all men are created equal. (Need I acknowledge that slaves and women were omitted from the formal definition here articulated and struggled mightily for inclusion?

But the general principle named both a partial and imperfect reality and a continuing aspiration.)

Many conservatives found an extension of equality beyond legal recognition balderdash because it was obvious to them that people were very different from one another, indeed, unequal by nature. Such persons equated equality with sameness; inequality with difference. Since it is clear, they insisted and continue to insist, that human beings differ, this means society must reflect those differences. We will invariably wind up with widespread social inequality because people are not the same; inequality is lodged in nature. It follows that attempts to alter institutions in order to eliminate or reduce inequality will require nasty social surgery because we must then eliminate human differences themselves. It seems best, according to this conservative argument, to allow natural differences — seen as inequalities — to work themselves out even if the result is a highly stratified, inegalitarian society in the social and economic sense, although we remain equal before the law.

Those who opposed this view, usually persons of the political left, insisted that it strained credulity to believe that all those who were well placed had fully earned it and that their power and privilege simply flowed from their being different — unequal — from the rest of us. Alas, the radical egalitarian response often got as tendentious as that of its ideological opposite. Rather than challenging the view of equality that equated it with "sameness," many critics implicitly embraced this idea: the more we were the same, the better. So they extolled a fuzzy or utopian notion of a world in which people were as indistinguishable from one another as happy peas in the egalitarian pod. Arguments defending the continuing necessity to assess the disparate value or merit of diverse human capacities, abilities, and achievements vanished like the early-morning dew in the sunlight's steady glare. I remember this quite well — remember the heated denunciations of "elitism" from my college compatriots in the 1960s when evaluations of merit and accomplishment were defended. Some argued then, and the argument, if anything, is even more vehemently pressed today, that standards themselves are somehow inherently anti-democratic.

This vision of a bland equality of sameness, promoted by many calling themselves egalitarians, some indebted to Marxism, some not, got satirized by the American writer, Kurt Vonnegut, Jr., in his short story "Harrison Bergeron," which appears in a collection called *Welcome to the Monkey House.* Vonnegut writes: "The year was 2081 and everybody was finally equal. They weren't only equal before God and the law. They were equal every which way. Nobody was smarter than anybody else. Nobody was better-looking than anybody else. Nobody was stronger or quicker than anybody else. All this equality was due to the 211th, 212th, and 213th Amendments to the Constitution, and to the unceasing vigilance of agents of the United States Handicapper General."[26]

In this delightfully ironic yet worrisome tale, Vonnegut portrays a future society in which all differences, all particular and unique human talents and gifts, have been compensated for downward in order to achieve the "equal society," in the belief that differences in themselves constitute inequalities. Thus ballet dancers, naturally gifted and trained to be lithe and limber, must dance with huge weights and irons on their legs. This guarantees that those who cannot be ballet dancers, who haven't the gift, won't feel upset because the ballet dancers, appropriately weighted down, can't leap any higher or move any more gracefully than they can. The world of perfect equality, one in which nobody is better at anything than anybody else, is at last attained! Of course, Vonnegut's fictional world is one none of us would care to inhabit. That, surely, is his point.

In education and the academy the harsh equation of equality with sameness led to a muddleheaded assault on any notion of distinctiveness or value. A variety of policies got proposed and in many places implemented. A "core curriculum," for example, was jettisoned on the presumption that the core was suited only for elitists and hampered individual liberty. Some institutions of higher learning gave up grading students altogether. Others moved to a pass/fail system, which comes to the same thing. Textbook publishers knowingly began to "dumb down" texts in history, science, and literature. In an understandable and justifiable urge to improve the lot of the many, the distinctiveness of the one was forgotten, even disdained.

Richard Rodriguez, in his poignant autobiography about growing up as the son of Mexican immigrant parents in California and becoming a "scholarship

kid," writes of the condescending paternalism he
encountered all too often at the hands of interven-
tionist egalitarians. Rodriguez's particular target is
affirmative action and his own official categoriza-
tion as a "minority" as part of educational efforts,
supposedly in his behalf. But he begins to notice a
few things and to grow increasingly disquieted.
First, he notices that, although he received an excellent parochial education, he is treated as a victim of
cultural deprivation: the working assumption, of
course, was that he was both ignorant and incapable
of defending himself. He notices that all sorts of
"allowances" get made for those Mexican-American
students who are both poor and poorly educated,
ill-prepared as they are, being pushed through the
system under the assumption that standards of merit
and achievement are themselves unfair impositions
by an Anglo majority on any and all minorities.

In the name of equality, in order to promote sex and
race "integration" and levelling, political radicals and
school administrators acted in ways that were, in fact,
deeply paternalistic. Here are Rodriguez's own words:

> The conspiracy of kindness became a conspiracy of
> uncaring. Cruelly, callously, admissions committees
> agreed to overlook serious academic deficiency. I knew
> students in college then barely able to read, students
> unable to grasp the function of a sentence. I knew
> nonwhite graduate students who were bewildered by
> the requirement to compose a term paper and who
> each day were humiliated when they couldn't
> compete with other students in seminars. . . . Not

surprisingly, among those students with very poor academic preparation, few completed their courses of study. Many dropped out, blaming themselves for their failure. One fall, six nonwhite students I knew suffered severe mental collapse. None of the professors who had welcomed them to graduate school were around when it came time to take them to the infirmary or the airport. And the university officials who so diligently took note of those students in their self-serving totals of entering minority students finally took no note of them when they left.[27]

Unsurprisingly, at the time of the publication of his work, there were concerted attempts to discredit Rodriguez as a stalking-horse for right-wing reaction; in this way his arguments could be ignored and the general inability on the left to tolerate diversity in the ranks of minority groups — presumably they should all think alike — was made evident. This situation, if anything, has grown more rather than less pronounced in the past decade.

Remember, these assumptions were undertaken with a grim determination to level, to promote a sameness, in the name of educational and civic equality. That was a decade ago in the United States. Consider, next, how quickly things change or, perhaps better put, how quickly the rhetoric of difference has supplanted the rhetoric of equality — perhaps the better to promote homogenizing ends. I recall my own shock at a conference on women and feminism — the year, I believe, was 1989 — when I listened to two and a half days of assaults on the very idea of equality. Equality meant "the same." Equality was the mark of masculinism. Equality was the stigma of heterosexism. It was pretty much every nasty thing you could think of and come up with a name for. Somehow even the Nazis got to be perverse egalitarians in their rush to exterminate the different.

Equality, I learned, meant "homologization with the male subject." As that was news to me, I decided I needed to ponder this matter further. The rush to eliminate equality from our political idiom and our political aspiration struck me as daft. Recognizing that democracy without equality is an impossible proposition, I got the uneasy feeling, one that remains with me to this day and has only been strengthened by recent celebrations of difference as a uniform and fixed group identity, that perhaps many of those immersed in what they call the "discourse of difference" are not so keen on constitutional democracy itself. One participant in the conference was quite candid about her disdain. What women should be about, she claimed, was celebrating their will to power. Perhaps one shouldn't be too concerned. Perhaps this distaste for democratic verities is primarily an academic exercise, radical playacting by a few individuals who would be appalled to see the implication of their own ideas fully worked out. Perhaps.

But there is room for worry. As George Kateb notes, "To want to believe that there is either a fixed majority interest or a homogenous group identity is not compatible with the premises of rights-based individualism."[28] Although I prefer to speak of democratic "individuality" rather than "individualism," Kateb's point seems to me well taken. To the extent citizens begin to retribalize into ethnic or other "fixed-identity groups," democracy falters. Any possibility for human dialogue, for democratic communication and commonality, vanishes as so much froth on the polluted sea of phony equality. Difference more and more becomes exclusivist. If you are black and I am white, by definition I do not and cannot, in principle, "get it." There is no way that we can negotiate the space between our pregiven differences. We are just stuck with them; stuck in what political thinkers used to call "ascriptive characteristics," things we cannot change about ourselves. Mired in the cement of our own identities, we need never deal with one another. Not really. One of us will win and one of us will lose the cultural war or the political struggle. That is what it is all about: power and nothing but power of the most reductive, impositional sort.

Political theorist Sheldon Wolin fears that that most important of all democratic categories — the citizen — will dissolve in the acids of this new ideology of difference, an ideology that despairs of, or huffily rejects, equality. Here Wolin is defining equality as "some broad measure of similarity if only to support a notion of membership that entails equality of rights, responsibilities, and treatment."[29] Repudiating the "sameness" of equality for its homogenizing urge, difference ideologues embrace their own version of sameness — an exclusionist sameness along lines of gender, race, ethnicity, and sexual preference. There is no apparent end to this process as identities get shaved off into more and more minute slivers, for example, lesbian women of colour, or some particular gay orientation by contrast to some other, or white men who were treated roughly by their fathers — the possibilities are endless. Ironically it has traditionally been the "nondemocratic rulers, the men who justify their rule by appealing to differences — heredity, divinity, merit, knowledge — who reduce populations to a common condition," Wolin writes.[30] We now impose a common condition on ourselves in the name of diversity.

If one sees in democratic principles, including the insistence that we are obliged to reach out to one another rather than to entrench in our isolated groups, only a cover for hidden privileges, one stalls out as a citizen. This tendency leads to a terrible impasse, Wolin concludes, one to which "the politics of difference and the ideology of multiculturalism have contributed by rendering suspect the language and possibilities of collectivity, common action, and shared purposes."[31] Yet, at the same time, those pushing such a politics must, in practice, make appeal to "some culture of commonality" in launching their demands that their differences be respected and their grievances responded to. There is, in fact, a way this can be done that recognizes both the "difference" and the commonality of an aggrieved group.

Here I call to attention the discourse of equality and difference as it pertains to the developmentally disabled. The best way to proceed in these matters is always through concrete example. I think here of my own daughter, a mildly retarded or, as we have come to say, "developmentally different" young adult.

I can track four stages in the story of equality and difference as it pertains to citizens with developmental disabilities. First, the "retarded" are construed as outside the world of equality altogether, having been identified by others as persons lacking the qualities necessary to play a part in the world of equality and inequality, the world of juridical and civic relations, the world of public freedom. Their difference here disqualifies them by definition. Some, of course, even put such persons outside the boundaries of humanity itself. Remember, it was the mentally handicapped and disabled who were the first targets of systematic Nazi extermination. In the second stage the "retarded," still called and thought of as such, are drawn within the circle of concern by those who do have a civic identity, who are part of the world of democratic equality. The disabled become the recipients of concern; their welfare must be seen to. But they are not yet participants in the drama of democratic equality themselves. In a third phase the "retarded," in and through their "normal" representatives, make claims upon the "equal," arguing that they, too, have the qualifications to be part of the discourse. They, too, can vote and hold jobs — or the vast majority can. So, over time, they are incorporated on the presumption that they are not so "different" as was once assumed. Finally persons with retardation, the developmentally different, find their own voice, however halting, and insist that they may not be human subjects in the

identical sense of those called "normal," but that
their difference does not sever them from equality.

The developmentally disabled are more like than
unlike the majority of persons in vital ways. But the
disabled also differ so they must struggle to make
the case for equality with respect for difference.
They seek recognition. Language shifts: We are not
"retards," they implore us. We are your fellow citizens with disabilities. Equality, or entering the discourse of equality, here does not and need not
conduce to homogeneity, to the "same." Instead,
equality remains a powerful term of political discourse and an instrument for social change and
justice, one of the strongest weapons the relatively
powerless have at their disposal in order to make
their case and define their aims *before* their fellow
citizens.

But if I have consigned equality to the discursive
trash heap as so much phony baloney, as we used to
say as children, and I scream at you that I will have
none of it; if, instead, I insist that what politics must
consist in is you acknowledging and recognizing my
differences but, at the same time, you are not allowed to engage me about these differences directly
because we have nothing to say to each other, then
I can only respond that you are not thinking and
acting like a democratic citizen. You are thinking
and acting like a royal pain in the neck, and the
sooner I can get you out of sight and mind, I will,
not because I am a racist or a sexist or a homophobe
or any of the other handy labels we toss around all
too easily these days, but because I am weary of

being accused of bad faith no matter what I do, or say, or refrain from doing or saying.

How did we get into this mess? There are many reasons, including the unravelling of democratic civil society I discussed in the first two chapters. Here I want to focus on another dimension to the trials of contemporary democracy: education. American public education is in big trouble and has been for at least two decades or more. Public school defenders are on the defensive. Most often they portray themselves as embattled champions of democracy against repressive right-wingers, evangelical hotheads, and irrational and unenlightened parents. Now there are no doubt repressive types and hotheads and overwrought parents engaged in skirmishes with educational institutions, from preschool through universities. But critics do not neatly fit this demeaning and misleading picture.

Bear in mind the following: it was taken for granted from the start of the American democratic experiment that the survival of the republic for any length of time would depend heavily on cultivating civic sentiments among the young. The optimistic hope was that national character itself could be formed by careful moulding of the children of each new generation. This hope had a long and noble lineage. Pericles in his funeral oration — I will discuss it in detail in my next chapter — marked the difference between the Spartan system that subjected young boys to harsh and laborious training replete with grim martial restrictions by contrast to Athenian generosity and leniency. We Athenians, he insisted, are just as brave as they are, but we are open, we promote goodwill and what today we might call "well roundedness." Small wonder Athens's citizens fall in love with her!

The indefatigable American Founders debated education, rejecting explicitly a classic civic republican education modelled on the Spartan example because it demanded and likely yielded homogeneity and sameness. In *Federalist Paper* Number 10 Publius advances a commitment to civility, one that implies acceptance of difference, as well as political equality. The "spirit of the people," informed by religious principles and a belief in nature and nature's laws, required no prefixed and dogmatic creed. This version of difference involved awareness of different opinions: we don't all think alike. The claims to difference were couched on an epistemological rather than an ontological level, by contrast to much contemporary multiculturalism with its vision of tribalistically exclusive groups given ontologically: this is what we *are*. According to this view, there is such a thing as "thinking black" or "thinking white." You can't help it, if you are one or the other. To the extent that public schools put themselves at the service of this latter version of multiculturalism, they disastrously abandon the turf they were deeded, the space within which they were enjoined to help create a commitment to a rough-and-ready social egalitarianism coupled with an equally strong commitment to civility.

But how can imposed uniformity — whether of sameness or difference — prepare citizens of a democracy to exercise civic and social responsibilities? This is a worry many now have about the educational wars being waged in America over so-called "multicultural" curricula that, in fact, entrench differences. For the new multiculturalism promotes what philosophers call "incommensurability." This means, quite literally, that if I am white and you are black, we cannot, in principle, speak to or understand each other. You just don't and won't "get it." As a form of ideological teaching, multicultural absolutism isolates us in our own skins and equates culture to racial or ethnic identity. Some have described this process as one of "resegregation." And they wonder: how long will it take before we move from separate approaches for, say, black children in the name of Afrocentricity, to a quest for entirely separate schools? The glory of American public education has been its mingling across class, gender, ethnicity, and race. That was part of the democratic ethos.

Democracy, if you will permit me yet another reminder, is not simply a set of procedures, a constitution, but an ethos, a spirit, a way of responding, a way of conducting oneself every day. Not being simple, democracy does not afford us a straightforward answer to the question of what education in, and for, democracy might be. If we move too quickly to the notion of relevance — teach them something practical so they can get jobs when they leave school — we may stress watery adaptation above authentic excellence. If we concentrate exclusively on the few, assuming that the many are less vital in the overall scheme of things, the democratic culture necessary to sustain constitutional democracy over the long haul will either wither on the vine or not bear fruit in the first place. If we say education must be for the many, and we believe the many are not up to much, we abandon excellence for a lowest common denominator: there goes Jefferson's aristocracy of virtue and talent!

There is a delicate line that separates over-politicization of education from an awareness of the fact that education is never outside a world of which politics — how human beings govern and order a way of life in common — is a necessary feature. Education is always cast as the means whereby some, or all, citizens of a particular society get their bearings and learn to live with and among one another. Education always reflects a society's views of what is excellent, worthy, necessary. These reflections are not cast in concrete, like so many foundation stones; rather, they are ongoingly refracted and reshaped as definitions, meanings, and purposes change through democratic contestation. In this sense education is political. But this is different from being directly and blatantly politicized, being made to serve interests and ends imposed by militant groups — whether in the name of heightened racial awareness, or true biblical morality, or androgyny, or therapeutic self-esteem, or all the other sorts of enthusiasms in which we are currently awash.

Consider the following examples. A class takes up the Declaration of Independence and the grand pronouncement that "All men are created equal." But women (and many men) were disenfranchised. Slaves were not counted as full persons. How could this be? What meaning of equality did the American

Founders embrace? Were any of them uneasy about this? How did they square this shared meaning with what we perceive to be manifest inequalities? What was debated and what was not? What political and moral exigencies of that historic moment compelled what sorts of compromises? Might things have gone differently? And so on. This I take to be an instance of reflective political education in and for a particular democracy — the American version — and our own perennial dilemma of the one and the many.

But let me put forward a second example, exaggerated in order to mark the differences between the two instances as clearly as I can. A teacher declares that nothing good ever came from the hand of that abstract, all-purpose villain, the "dead, white European male." The words and deeds of such men, including the Founders, are nefarious. They were nothing but racists and patriarchalists, blatant oppressors who hid behind fine-sounding words. All they created is tainted and hypocritical. There is no ambiguity. Here the matter simply ends. All is foreclosed. All has been exposed. The world closes in. Debate ends or is discouraged. To express a different point of view is to betray one's own false consciousness, venality, or white, patriarchal privilege.

This attitude I take to be an instance of unreflective, dogmatic politicization. It evades the dilemmas of democratic equality rather than offering us points of critical reflection on that dilemma. This sort of education fails in its very particular and important task of preparing us for a world of ambiguity and variety. It equips us only for resentment. Let me be clear: I am not here indicting education, whether public or private, elementary, secondary, or college level, for our growing balkanization. But I am suggesting that the schools, which once took as their mission the instilling of some measure of commonality across differences, now suffer under the claim that that effort itself was but another name for "normalization" and cultural imperialism. All those dedicated teachers in all those public schools, working long hours for not very good pay, seeing their work as a vocation, are now relegated by some to the status of agents of domination, sometimes witting, sometimes not.

There are two off-kilter positions, then. In one the mesmerized worshipper of authority, who will brook no criticism of the Founders, only adulation, denies himself the critical freedom that is rightly his as an educator, and necessary to impart to his students; in the second, the agitated negator of all that has gone before preaches freedom from the dismal and spurious past, from a tradition she would cast off and can see only as all-pervasive and menacing, and her students better see it that way, too. But a genuine education in and for democracy is one that brings matters to the surface, helps us to engage in a debate with interlocutors long dead or protagonists who never lived save on the page and, through that engagement, to elaborate alternative conceptions through which to apprehend our world and the way that world represents itself.

"Perhaps," writes the political philosopher Michael Oakeshott, "we may think of the components of culture as voices, each the expression of a distinct condition and understanding of the world and a distinct idiom of human self-understanding, and of the culture itself as these voices joined, as such voices could only be joined, in a conversation — an endless unrehearsed intellectual adventure in which, in imagination, we enter into a variety of modes of understanding the world and ourselves and are not disconcerted by the differences or dismayed by the inconclusiveness of it all."[32] This openness to diverse voices helps to keep alive both our distinctiveness and the possibility of commonalities.

I think of my own education, and my democratic dreams, as they were nurtured in the rural Colorado village in which I grew up. The Timnath Public School, District Number 62, incorporated grades 1 to 12 in a single building: there weren't that many of us. I remember that we memorized the Declaration of Independence and the Gettysburg Address. The Gettysburg Address recitation, when my classmates and I were in grades 7 and 8, a single classroom under the firm if somewhat eccentric tutelage of Miss McCarthy, was always quite an event. We would line up in a single row around the classroom. On Miss McCarthy's signal we would begin to hum the stirring song of the American Civil War, "The Battle Hymn of the Republic," as Miss McCarthy recited the Gettysburg Address with flourish and fervour. She had a way of trailing off each sentence in a trembly, melodramatic whisper that sometimes left we hummers in stitches. But I never forgot the Gettysburg Address and its promise of democratic equality.

My democratic dream was nurtured by a presumption that none of us was stuck inside our own skins; that our identities and our ideas were not reducible to our membership in a race, an ethnic group, or a sex. I remember my father telling me that the "Mexican kids" — Mexican being the term of respect in that time and place — were sometimes smart and nice and sometimes not, just like other kids. Before Martin Luther King made it the central theme of his great "I Have a Dream" speech, I had already learned that I was to judge others, not by the colour of their skins but by the content of their character. It would never have occurred to me that I should "think girlishly" or that my friend Raymond Barros was required to think "with his blood."

By the time we reached high school in that isolated little place, our text for English class was called *Adventures in Reading*. I still have my copy, having purchased it from the school because I loved so many of the stories and poems it contained. The table of contents was divided into "Good Stories Old and New," with such bracing subsections as "Winning Against the Odds," "Meeting the Unusual," and "Facing Problems." We read "Lyrics from Many Lands" and "American Songs and Sketches." I looked at this text recently as I thought about democracy and education. By no means was this a book dominated by a single point of view, that of the dreaded dead white European male. We read Mary O'Hara, Dorothy Canfield, Margaret Weymouth Jackson, Elsie Singmaster, Selma Lagerlöf, Rosemary Vincent Benét, Kathryn Forbes, Sarojini

Naidu, Willa Cather, Emily Dickinson, on and on. We read the great abolitionist Frederick Douglass and the black reformer Booker T. Washington. We read Leo Tolstoy and Pedro de Alarcón. We read translations of Native American warrior songs.

Now this reading wasn't done under the specific rubric of multiculturalism. But it was undertaken in the assumption that life is diverse, filled with many wonders. Through *Adventures in Reading* we could make the lives and thoughts of others somehow, in some way, our own. In my imaginings and yearnings I didn't feel constrained because some of those I most admired were men. I later chafed against the constraints that lay outside my imagination, of course, but education is about opening the world up, not imprisoning us in terms of race, gender, or ethnicity. I was taught: "Reading is your passport to adventure in faraway places. In books the world lies before you, its paths radiating from great cities to distant lands, to scenes forever new, forever changing. . . . Reading knows no barrier, neither time nor space nor bounds of prejudice — it admits us all to the community of human experience." Clearly I was a lucky child, a lucky *democratic* child, for I learned that, in Oakeshott's words, "Learning is not merely acquiring information . . . nor is it merely 'improving one's mind'; it is learning to recognize some specific invitations to encounter particular adventures in human self-understanding."[33]

This work of human self-understanding can be neither the exclusive purview of the family nor of some overweening state or bureaucracy, whether it is pushing homogeneity or multiculturalism. It is primarily a task of civil society, of which schools are a part. Of course, education in and for a democratic culture is a porous affair, open to the wide world outside the door and beyond the playground, but that does not mean it must needs become the playing of purveyors of passing enthusiasms, whether political or pedagogical. The danger in continuing down our present path is that our understanding of education itself is increasingly imperiled because we have done too little to protect education, and the child being educated, from heavy-handed intrusion by those who would have both education and child serve this political master or that ideological purpose. Thus, we increasingly give over to education all sorts of tasks it is ill-equipped to handle. At the same time we seem intent on stripping education of what, in fact, it ought to be about: that invitation to particular "adventures in human self-understanding," in Oakeshott's terms.

A democratic drama is the playing out of the story of self-limiting freedom. The danger in any ideological definition of education is that it undermines this essential dimension, in much the way Pericles argued that Sparta undermined authentic, because self-chosen, civic bravery by mandating harsh and severe sacrifice. Because democracy is the political form that permits and requires human freedom as responsibility, any definition or system that sanctions evasion of responsibility, as I sink my identity totally into that of a group and its "group think," imperils democracy. Whether in the name of change or to forestall change, an ideological system of education is the worst possible way for human beings to try to order and to ensure their collective democratic affairs. For once a world of personal responsibility with its characteristic virtues and marks of decency (honour, friendship, fidelity, fairness) is ruptured or emptied, what rushes in to take its place is politics as a "technology of power," in Václav Havel's phrase. Responsibility, according to Havel — and he is as surefooted a guide as any currently available — flows from the aims of life "in its essence," these being plurality and independent self-constitution as opposed to the conformity, uniformity, and stultifying dogmas of left- and right-wing ideologues who abandon reality and assault life with their rigid, abstract chimeras.

A fusion of freedom and responsibility yields a distinct but definite political conclusion: democracy is the political form that permits and requires human freedom, not as an act of self-overcoming, nor pure reason, but in service to others in one's own time and place. That is why we are so concerned with education, with children getting acquainted with the world in a way that helps them, too, to assume responsibility. To live "within the truth," as Havel calls it, is to give voice to a self, and a citizen, that has embraced responsibility for the here and now. As he writes, "That means that responsibility is ours, that we must accept it and grasp it here, now, in this place where the Lord has set us down, and that we cannot lie our way out of it by moving somewhere else, whether it be to an Indian ashram or to a parallel *polis*."[34]

Havel believes we are living in the midst of a general crisis of human consciousness, in West and East, in North and South. That crisis manifests itself in the spheres of human freedom, responsibility, and identity itself. Acceptance of the risks of free action — an affirmation education in and for democracy makes possible, although it does not guarantee — makes one a person and forms the basis of one's identity. Any mode of thought or program of education that reduces human responsibility narrows the horizon of human possibility. To assume "full responsibility" is not to lapse into dour moralism, nor to universalize a giddy and boundless compassion, but to take up the specific, concrete burdens of one's own culture. Education that undermines even the possibility that at least some among us may be called upon to bear witness is an exercise in speciousness.

This is tough stuff. But, then, democracy is for the stout of heart who know there are things worth fighting for in a world of paradox, ambiguity, and irony. This democratic way — moderation with courage, open to compromise from a basis of principle — is the rare but now and then attainable fruit of the democratic imagination and, in action, the democratic citizen. But there have always been skeptics. If democracy is on trial in our time, beleaguered by foes and bedeviled by friends, democracy was both tried and condemned by a number of my distinguished forebears in the world of Western political philosophy. Perhaps it is worth making a brief detour into democracy's shady past in order to take the most accurate measure we can of current democratic prospects.

IV

DEMOCRACY'S SHADY PAST

STEPPING BACK FOR A MOMENT from democracy's contemporary trials will help us to recall what might be called democracy's perpetual trial. Although democracy enjoys a good press as we enter the waning years of the twentieth century, it has not always been so. The history of Western politics and Western political thought puts on display a variety of powerful arguments both for and against democracy. While it is the case that nowadays no one wants to be thought "anti-democratic," including tyrants, oligarchs, and zealots of whatever stripe, this is a relatively recent development. To call oneself a democrat in previous epochs was to court suspicion, even disdain. In our own enthusiasm for the word *democracy*, we not only downplay anti-democratic developments in our own societies, we forget just how hard-fought the struggle over democracy has been, in texts and assemblies, in schools and streets, in the homes of the bereft and the corridors of power alike.

I ask the reader to return with me to the time and place where the issues at stake between democrats and anti-democrats first got joined: ancient Attica. Modern political philosophers and citizens alike look to our ancient Greek forebears as the originating fathers of democracy; indeed, we are taught that the Athenians "invented" democracy. But, by our contemporary reckoning, it was a rather peculiar democracy: the vast majority of the populace of Athens could neither vote nor deliberate in assembly, nor, indeed, fight in a war — the signal responsibility and privilege of the citizen. Slaves, labourers, and women were excluded. Nonetheless, the Athenians proclaimed themselves a special sort of breed, that called by the name "democrat," because the minority who were citizens had final say on the actions to be taken by the *polis*, the political community, as a whole.

The term *democracy* was known as early as the seventh century B.C. By the second half of the sixth century, arguments for and against democracy had jelled. As the story is usually told, democrats won the fight for the "hearts and minds" of later generations, including early modern social contract thinkers, constitutionalists, and political reformers seeking ancient lineage for, and classical legitimation of, many of their own ideas. One need look no further than the American *Federalist Papers* to read the assessments of the pros and cons of democracy, ancient and modern, taken up by the founders of the American republic. The Founders were well aware of the classical democratic heritage. But they also appreciated the fact that an ancient political philosopher had the better argument — or at least the most elegantly elaborated case — and it was anti- rather than pro-democratic. This argument was deeded to later generations by the masterful pen of Plato, the Athenian.[35]

But let us take up the pro-democratic story first, especially as it was articulated in the fullness of rhetorical splendour in the funeral speech of Pericles, a leader in Athens's prolonged conflict with Sparta. The Peloponnesian War convulsed Athens, her allies, and her opponents for nearly thirty years in the fifth century B.C. Pericles' speech has come down to us as it was reconstructed by the great historian of that war, Thucydides. Remember, as backdrop to his speech, that arguments for and against democracy had long raged. During the sixth and fifth centuries B.C., many Greek city-states had attained rough-and-ready democratic constitutions, founded on the premise of equality or *isonomia*, the condition said to pertain between and among citizens in whom ultimate sovereign authority was lodged and who determined the course of their city's fate by majority vote.

In Athens this system had been nearly perfected: an Assembly of the people deliberated, with all who were citizens participating. Who ruled over or governed the Assembly was not permanent but shifting; a selected leader was first among equals, and his position was not a permanent leasehold but a temporary obligation and honour. All citizens could speak freely in the Assembly as part of the lawmaking process. To its proponents, democracy — the rule of the people — was a glory indeed, a shining example of the liberation of the citizen from the toils of everyday life, the world of necessity, in order that he might enjoy the brisk and bracing freedom of the political realm.[36] ⚘

Pericles used the occasion of the burial of Athenian war dead to proffer his paean to Athenian democracy. All later democrats embraced this effort as the most splendid example of *epideictic* oratory, speeches made for public occasions imbued with an explicit political content. In ancient democracy words reigned supreme — those words uttered to and before one's fellow citizens, most importantly, but to all Athenians, the people or *demos* in general, on the solemn occasions of the burial of war dead. Nicole Loraux, a classical scholar, goes so far as to claim that Athenian democracy got "invented" through rhetoric, especially the funeral oration, a practice not only proper to but peculiar to that premier democratic city, Athens. "In and through the funeral oration," she writes, "democracy becomes . . . a name to describe a model city."[37]

Why, then, is Pericles' great speech taken as exemplary? Because he uses the ritual of burying the first war dead in the struggle against Sparta to do more, much more, than honour those who "shall not have died in vain," in the words of a nineteenth-century funeral oration, Abraham Lincoln's Gettysburg Address, very much modelled after the ancient example. Pericles uses his oration to define and to refine Athenian democracy and to explain why sacrifice in her name was a worthy and noble thing. He emphasizes the uniqueness of Athens; not simply the constitution and the laws but those qualities of mind and habit that define what it means to belong to this democratic city. Athenians are not, like the Spartans, forced by a "painful discipline" to conform. Rather, they are self-conscious citizens and patriots. The dead have chosen the city over their own lives.

Pericles defines democracy for the gathered assembly, including mothers and fathers there to bury their beloved sons, in these words: "Our constitution is called a democracy because power is in the hands not of a minority but of the whole people. When it is a question of settling private disputes, everyone is equal before the law; when it is a question of putting one person before another in positions of public responsibility, what counts is not membership of a particular class, but the actual ability which the man possesses."

But there is something other than just the more or less codified, legal provisos of a democratic way of life as laid out in the constitution or *politeia*. Pericles extols the "day-to-day" relations of Athenians with "each other," the practices and spirit of the people. For, he says, we "do not get into a state with our next-door-neighbor if he enjoys himself in his own way, nor do we give him the kind of black looks which, though they do no real harm, still do hurt people's feelings. We are free and tolerant in our private lives; but in public affairs we keep the law. This is because it commands our deep respect." It is the "laws themselves" that are obeyed, including the "unwritten laws which it is an acknowledged shame to break. We Athenians love beauty; we are open to

the glory of words and deeds; our city is an education to Greece; future ages will honor us." Therefore,
he tells the grieving crowd, "Fix your eyes every day
on the greatness of Athens, as she really is, and . . .
fall in love with her." Freedom depends on courage
and honour. The dead offer us examples of both.[38]

These are stirring words. They reflect the sort of
oratory we Americans used to expect on Independence Day and other civic holidays when those
occasions were not just an opportunity to play golf
or go fishing or watch television. In the past they
were opportunities to recite and listen to the
words of the Declaration of Independence and
that unparalleled example of American political
oratory, Lincoln's Gettysburg Address, in which
he extolled a government of, by, and "for the people" and prayed that it would never "perish from
the earth."

Plato, it must be said, will have none of this. A
reminder of what democracy entailed — of what
fuelled Plato's ire — is perhaps useful before we
take the measure of his powerful discontents in this
matter. Ancient democracy affirmed the "sovereign
power of the *demos* with a recognition of majority
law, based on the equality of the citizens."[39] This
equality meant, remember, equality in the *agora*, the
open place where citizens assembled and debated,
where rhetoric took primacy. Government was not
by *all* the people, given the restrictions of citizenship, but it must be for the people. For her defenders,
like Pericles, democracy is the name given to the
model city in which the power of the people and of

law, political liberty and freedom of speech, political equality and rotation of offices and, above all, justice between and among citizens, defined political life. Lincoln took his own stab at offering a brief definition in the form of an elegant two sentences on democracy in 1858. He wrote: "As I would not be a *slave*, so I would not be a *master*. This expresses my idea of democracy. Whatever differs from this, to the extent of the difference, is no democracy."[40] Lincoln, the master rhetorician and writer of American democracy, knew a good turn of phrase and coined many himself.

Plato, as I have already noted, would not be pleased. He wasn't happy with democrats in his own time and he would no doubt be appalled by ours. Lincoln's democratic sentiments and his search for the nobility of the common man would drive Plato to despair. Had not a corrupt Athenian democracy put to death that noblest of men, the philosopher Socrates? "With all due respect, Mr. Lincoln," he might write, "your definition of democracy is not nearly so airtight, not the ringing bell echoing through the stillness of a glorious, unending democratic sunrise, stirring the hearts of all who hear the sound, as you appear to believe. Democracy, the American experiment, the 'last best hope on earth'? Count me out," I hear Plato grumble, and I imagine him going on to chide Mr. Lincoln for the too literal definition Lincoln proffers of "slave" and "master," hence of democracy itself.

"You seem to think," Plato might say to Honest Abe, "that slavery is merely a matter of ownership in another where one — the slave — is legally and politically unfree and the other — the master — enjoys his freedom, including the freedom to own the slave and to benefit from his unpaid labour, labour that frees the master for other, nobler pursuits. But the subjection of some is, in fact, a precondition for the only authentic freedom — the freedom not so much of the master as of the wise and virtuous person. In my ideal city I call these paragons Guardians, for they are those who have defeated the worst slavery, their own slavery to baser instincts and passions. The actual indenture of the corrupted many to the wise few is a matter of little consequence by contrast to the wholly legitimate triumph by the few over those baser passions that enslave the many and suit them only to an inferior status."

Lincoln, hearing this, would no doubt tweak Plato a bit, a twinkle in his eye, as I hear him intone in that high-pitched Kentucky–Illinois nasal drawl said to characterize his speech, "Why, Mr. Plato, I fear no one has delved deeper into the well of knowledge than you appear to have done and come up dryer. How can one know, save through democratic give-and-take, the rough-and-tumble of politics itself, who is wisest and who is best? Who is the slave to passion and who possesses the wisdom to govern?" Let us imagine Mr. Lincoln leaving the room at this point and giving Plato the floor. Lincoln has other things to tend to, perhaps writing the Gettysburg Address for delivery to those who have gathered to honour the dead of the terrible civil war convulsing the American republic.

What is Plato so exercised about? Why is he considered the most potent of all anti-democratic philosophers to this day? Why, indeed, is it the case that among political philosophers, democracy has never enjoyed the unambiguous good press it has long received among ordinary citizens, in the West and much of the world, a world now witness to all sorts of dramatic transformations that go by the name "democracy" and march to democracy's tune, understood as self-determination, self-respect, and a recognition of human rights? Well, it must be said, Plato's fears are many. For him democracy is dangerous; it represents a derangement of the right order of things. To evaluate Plato's sustained screed against democracy, let us, briefly, take the measure of ancient deliberation of the systematic or philosophic sort about democracy.

The Greeks reckoned democracy one of the possible political forms or constitutions. Being fond of typologies, the Greeks enumerated the characteristics of different constitutions and then ranked them from best to worst. Plato goes along with the typologies of forms of constitutions and, of these forms in their noncorrupt varieties, democracy is ranked lowest. In his masterwork of the political imagination, *The Republic*, Plato stresses the degenerate forms and democracy is degenerate indeed.

Plato's case against democracy, presented in the words of Socrates, is philosophical, epistemological, and political. The political argument is stark and simple: democracy deteriorates into "licence" as people do whatever they want whenever something much lower in Plato's ranking of human possibilities than "the spirit" moves them. All sorts of unchecked dispositions are given free rein. Rhetoricians, cast by Plato, through Socrates' words, as unscrupulous men who manipulate through speech, take over the souls of the young through "false and boasting speeches and opinions . . ." True speech is banished, the authentic gold driven out by the tinny dross of what is pleasing and popular.

Let us listen to the precise terms of the excoriation — the reference point here is the rhetoricians, purveyors of cheap democratic faith of the most corrupt sort. "Once they have emptied and purged [the good] from the soul of the man whom they are seizing," says Plato, "they proceed to return insolence, anarchy, wastefulness, and shamelessness from exile, in a blaze of light, crowned and accompanied by a numerous chorus, extolling and flattering them by calling insolence good education; anarchy, freedom; wastefulness, magnificence; and shamelessness, courage."[41]

Not a pretty picture. These corrupted democratic speechifiers and their minions are idle, they neglect everything, they engage in politics by jumping up and down over transient enthusiasms, they want to make a lot of money, and they seek to gratify all desires instantly. In this hellish world purchased slaves and men and women become free in identical ways, another sign of the ultimate in freedom as licence and moral turpitude.

That is the political story. But behind it lies a denunciation by Plato of political rhetoric, the echoing resonances of the spoken word aimed explicitly at democratic ends. Behind it also lies an epistemology that denigrates "mere opinion," which is available to, and indeed the base lifeblood of the many, by contrast to that true knowledge of the transcendent Forms achieved only by the wise. Disheartened with the treatment sometimes accorded just men on this earth, Plato would create a world in which the just man is not only secure from the hounds baying at his heels but in which that man, and others of his kind, hold absolute power. Plato would preclude the debate and controversy of those heated assemblies: these invite only chaos and discord. The wise, however, know one can attain certitude and finality only through a complex dialectic that leads to transcendent and unchanging Truth. Plato seeks a few good men — Philosophers — to rule. These wise few, who have glimpsed and made their own true knowledge, must serve as physicians called upon to treat the terrible sickness of society.

Plato sharply divides rhetoric from dialectic, opinion from knowledge. The high-minded search for truth looks nothing like those forensic feats in the Athenian Assembly, or even Pericles' funeral oration. Plato's dialectic of knowledge is set up in opposition to a democratic rhetoric of persuasion. He tackles those called Sophists who plied rhetoric professionally by calling them mere panderers. In the Platonic dialogue that bears the name of Socrates' hapless interlocutor, a rhetorician called Gorgias, Socrates manoeuvres Gorgias into declaiming that speech-making is not concerned with helping the

"sick" — the vast multitude to whom Plato's physi-
cian would bring philosophic and political health —
learn how to live in order to become well; no, it
involves only freedom for oneself, the power of
ruling by convincing others to concur with one's
argument. Gorgias is trapped by Socrates into admitting that oratory is not about right or wrong but
mere persuasion, a "spurious counterfeit of a branch
of the art of government," that branch called by the
name "democracy."[42]

Democracy in Plato's scheme of things contains
no authentic or meaningful speech, only the babble
of the ignorant. The ignorant are stuck in mere opinion and give in to base instinct. Hope lies with the
few or, as Plato puts it, "the more decent few" who
can master desire. From this "smallest group,"
which comes to share in the only knowledge legiti-
mately called "wisdom," a city may arise "worthy
of the philosophic nature."[43] Plato has a cure. He
elaborates it in his "ideal city," *The Republic*. Whether
he hoped for its actual implementation is, of course,
unclear: most subsequent philosophers think he
held forth no such prospect. Some even suggest he
was being ironic about the whole business. But later
anti-democrats took his arguments to heart, some
aspiring themselves to be among the few public-
spirited men who ruled for the common good.

A brand-new order, one free from the corrupt
democratic taint, is a hard thing to attain: Plato
acknowledges this at the outset and throughout his
text. The people are so easily misled and aroused.
Thus, wise rulers must forbid speeches about the

gods and expunge all tall tales of ancient heroes, for poetry inflames the many. The ruler must lie for the benefit of the city. If the ideal city is to come into being, says Plato, rulers must take "the dispositions of human beings; as though they were a tablet — which, in the first place, they would wipe clean. And that's hardly easy."[44] Although Plato appears to want us to have empathy with the arduous task faced by his rulers, a more likely response is concern for who or what is to get "wiped clean." As well, the achievement of a just state, a perfect anti-democracy, requires the creation of such a powerful, all-encompassing bond between individuals and the state that all social and political conflict disappears, discord melts away, and the state comes to resemble a "single person," a fused, nigh organic entity.

Away, then, with private marriage, family life and child-rearing, at least for the Guardian class, which must have no competing loyalties other than its wise devotion to, and rule over, the city. A systematic meritocracy must prevail in which children are shunted about like raw material to be turned to the good of the unified city. It works like this: children from the lower orders of society, those stuck in the mire of ignorance, may perchance show discernible sparks of future wisdom. If so, that child must be removed from his or her parents at once, "without the smallest pity," and trained to be one of the brightest and the best.

Plato's explicit purpose with this social engineering is to prevent the emergence of hereditary oligarchies and to ensure the continuation of rule by the best. Thus, a system of eugenics is devised among his Guardians to match up males and females with their most likely mates in order that vigorous, healthy offspring will result. Immediately after birth the baby is removed from its biological mother and sent to a central nursery where it is entrusted to experts for its rearing. Guardian women who have given birth do nurse infants but are not allowed to nurse their *own* infants. Instead each mother nurses the anonymous baby presented to her when she enters the segregated children's quarter of the city. Should a mother get to know her own infant, she would have a private loyalty at odds with her unitary bond to the city; moreover, should the infant be one of the lesser sort, it must be sent "down" to the lower orders and a mother attached to an infant would make a huge ruckus about such a necessary move. Plato wants no messes in this Guardian encampment.

Well, this system is stern medicine indeed, and singularly unattractive to the democratic temperament. Yet it is precisely that temperament that Plato denigrates and would eradicate. Why? What is all the wrenching he proposes for? What does he fear? The only solution Plato sees to individual malaise and social corruption is a thoroughgoing, rationalized world in which individuals get slotted into niches along predetermined and unchanging criteria: are they up to the task of attaining wisdom, of moving beyond mere opinion, or not? Private homes and sexual attachments, devotion to friends, dedication to individual aims and purposes militate against single-minded devotion to the ideal city or a quest for Truth.

We see in Plato's strictures that disparagement of rhetoric goes hand in hand with disdain for the vulgar unseemliness of democratic politics. It is a bone in his throat that the wisest and best may not rule over those less wise and less noble. But we also see displayed what might be called the prototypical anti-democratic fear — the fear that things will easily fall apart if a city is divided instead of one. There are words scattered throughout *The Republic* that evoke a sense of chaos and disintegration: *asunder, destroy, dissolves, overwhelms, splits, evil.* And other terms are designated as potent enough to prevent the anarchy that democracy leads to: *dominate, censor, expunge, conform, bind, make one.* For Plato, every conflict is a potential cataclysm; every discussion in which differences are stated a threat portending disintegration; every sally an embryonic struggle unto death; every distinction a possible blemish on the canvas of harmonious and unsullied order.

Fear of disorder is a major hand, even a trump card, for anti-democrats historically. Taking a cue from Plato, later thinkers, devoted to the idea that there must be one overarching truth in a political system, one final voice, one unifying will, fretted excitedly about the anarchy they saw lurking, even smirking menacingly in the dark shadows of sunny democratic vistas. The democratic commitment to political freedom stirs up ceaseless disputation, they cry. The democratic devotion to *isonomia*, the principle of equality, riles the man or woman who looks with envy on his or her neighbour and wants "the same," for that is how equality is understood by ordinary folk, they warn. History teaches us that popular rages of all kinds flow from this construal, or misconstrual, of what democratic equality requires or demands.

A moderated way of working this problem out was elaborated by Aristotle, a philosopher far more friendly to democracy than Plato but still wary. Aristotle distinguished between good and bad constitutions: each good constitution can degenerate into a bad form. Democracy, Aristotle claimed, is the corrupt form of popular government. It is corrupt because within it the mass of people, the poor, take over and do so in a way likely to lead to violence and anarchy as laws are abandoned and unchecked self-interest triumphs. A right constitution, for Aristotle, is directed to the common interest — whether it is a monarchy or a *politeia*, a constitution of and for the people. But a bad or perverted constitution is captured by selfish interests, whether of a few or the majority. For Aristotle this is baneful, since the end of the state is not "mere life" but a "good life" and a good life is one of felicity and fairness.[45]

Plato's successor as the greatest of Greek philosophers, Aristotle feared democracy as a form of mobocracy, but he also rejected his revered predecessor's solution to that fear because, so Aristotle claimed, Plato's cure would be worse than the disease. His ideal city would produce a bad form of unity, lead to one-man rule, and ignore justice. For this reason Aristotle is often turned to as an antidote to Plato's stringently anti-democratic creed, despite his own misgivings in this matter. At this point I want to take up the worries and words of one more anti-democrat who numbers among the handful of universally acknowledged great political philosophers in the Western tradition — Thomas Hobbes.

Hobbes, from his sixteenth-century vantage point, held that a society could be run on a single principle: recognition that human beings are isolated monads driven by appetite and aversion. Hobbes's central concern was order. The manner in which he conceived alternatives — either anarchy or absolutism — precluded any consideration of other possibilities and, as we have already noticed with Plato, is characteristic of those who fear democracy. The threat of destruction is the basis of the Hobbesian solution to the problem of order on all levels and in each arena of human intercourse. Even the hapless child in the family agrees to be ruled absolutely, in effect signs a coercive contract, from fear of death at the hands of his parents. All human beings for Hobbes are anxious, fearful, threatening to themselves and others, full of inherent destructive passions. Hobbes views life before the creation of commonwealths as a terrifying and conflict-ridden state of nature, a "war of all against all," in his famous, or infamous, words.

To protect ourselves from death at the hands of our neighbour or a restless marauder, we make a deal — we agree to be ruled absolutely by a sovereign, Leviathan by name, whose powers are awesome. Indeed, he is an all-powerful earthly lord, one who enjoys the strength conferred on him by all others, who reduces all particular wills "unto one Will" in order that there might be a "reall Unitie of them all, in one and the same Person. . . . This is the Generation of that Mortall God, to which wee owe under the Immortall God, our peace and defense." This mortal God may judge all opinions, name all names, defend all things as "necessary to Peace, thereby to prevent Discord and Civill Warre."[46] There is a terrible equality in Hobbes's world, but it is not the democratic ideal; rather, it is the equality of the fearful, the equality of human beings so similar in power that any may kill another, for the less strong can make up for their difference in brawn by grabbing a bludgeon and bashing their neighbour's brains out as he sleeps.

Hobbes suggests to all who find this a distressing, even repellent view of the human condition and its prospects that we take a look around, consider how much we fear, and muse on what price we would pay were we caught up in a world of hideous dislocations, sudden and violent death, and rampaging ne'er-do-wells. Throughout our history, perceiving such Hobbesian realities, there are those who have sought, and others who have imposed, Hobbesian solutions. In his own way Hobbes is a utopian — one who believed that a dramatic move to create an all-powerful sovereign could rescue humanity from its travail. His solution is by no means democratic, but at least one could sleep at night. Peace comes at a heavy price.

But not all anti-democrats are disdainful of democracy, as was Plato, or scared out of their wits by it, as was Hobbes. There are others — syndicalists, romantic utopians, revolutionary socialists, some existentialists — for whom democracy is to be repudiated because it is so pitiful, an exercise in bourgeois banality in which the bland lead the bland down the narrow pathway of cultural conformism and self-interest wrongly understood, as all self-interest, in the long run, is bound to be. Democracy is for the faint-of-heart, the womanish, the effeminate. (The gendered terms of derision are used here knowingly, for one continuing gripe about democracy is that it negates the possibility for heroic action of the manly sort. The man — in Latin, *vir* — gets few opportunities to put on public display his *virtú* — his ability to get things done with aplomb and heroic savoir faire.)

Machiavelli mumbled in this way, being in the mould of energetic civic republicans that cherished the autonomy of the city but held out few hopes for a democratic constitution of the sort we moderns would recognize. Rousseau, following suit, held up Sparta as his great ancient exemplar, anti-democratic Sparta with its martial valour, not Athenian democracy with its public speech and equality between citizens. Although Rousseau is often numbered among the great democratic thinkers, his martial enthusiasms and insistence that the polity must be as one, that the national will must not be divided, that the citizen takes on an altogether new identity as his very will and person become part of "the common," suggests a monistic

drive ill-suited to the democratic temperament. Remember Pericles' funeral admonition: democracy is
about more than the constitution and laws; it is
about the habits and dispositions and everyday doings of a people.

That the everyday doings of ordinary people
should be taken into account, even accorded some
political weight and respect, drives utopians around
the bend. Twentieth-century revolutionaries, many
of them Marxist in their orientation and faith, turned
very ugly indeed in their attempt to create a unitary
order, a utopia cured of capitalist perfidy and democratic hypocrisy. Pity the poor bourgeois house-
holder, they moaned. He will disappear and his
wife, too, by contrast to the militant, the revolutionary, with his enemies to expose, foes to fight, his
world in which whole peoples must triumph or
vanish.

If your aim is a unitary order, a perfect regime in
which all good things coexist in perpetuity, the give
and take of democracy is thin gruel indeed. Lenin
and Hitler alike held democracy in contempt. Lenin
celebrated the coming of the First World War as a
way to cleanse the world of pathetic, petit bourgeois
bacilli. So did many of his ideological opponents on
the other side of the political spectrum: a great European war promised purging and redemption to
anti-democratic intellectuals and activists of the left
and the right. A group called the Futurists, aesthetes
devoted to purification through violence, shared
Lenin's contempt for the bourgeois world and his
conviction that its destruction must be ruthless and

total if reconstruction is to be permanent. War, they proclaimed, would wipe out "moralism, feminism, every opportunistic or utilitarian cowardice."[47] Democracy, of course, is the political expression of that despised cowardice in fulminations of this sort, past and present.

We hear similar proclamations today. I have already noted the disdain for democratic moderation and coalition-building on the part of some contemporary celebrants of multiculturalism and group difference. Those loudly and violently promoting the virtues of ethnic nationhood hate democracy. Religious fundamentalists who insist that politics must be theocratic find democracy the work of the devil. Ideologues who enjoin a world "beyond compromises" scorn democracy as anemic. They want the world to conform to their grandiose scheme.

This quest for a unitary order, a utopia, has been cast from Plato to the present as an argument against democracy, even if what the utopian claims to seek is a more complete, full, or authentic democracy. As Isaiah Berlin reminds us: "Utopias . . . are static. Nothing in them alters, for they have reached perfection: there is no need for novelty or change; no one can wish to alter a condition in which all natural human wishes are fulfilled. The assumption on which this is based is that men have a certain fixed, unaltering nature, certain universal, common, immutable goals. Once these goals are realized, human nature is wholly fulfilled. The very idea of universal fulfillment presupposes that human beings as such seek the same essential goals, identical for all, at all times, everywhere. For unless this is so, Utopia cannot be Utopia, for then the perfect society will not perfectly satisfy everyone."[48]

The utopian tells us that once the struggle is over all will be well; either problems themselves will have vanished in the blissful harmony of a perfect order or that problems will somehow be solved without decisive conflict, with some walking away dissatisfied at the outcome. Democrats know better; indeed, democracy is precisely an institutional, cultural, habitual way of acknowledging the pervasiveness of conflict and the fact that our loyalties are not one, our wills are not single, our opinions are not uniform, our ideals are not cut from the same cloth.

Despite all this, despite the blood shed on the altar of various ahistoric abstractions — and utopias are always abstract pictures of a shimmering future someday graspable but not yet reachable because enemies and the benighted and self-interested stand in the way of their realization — the anti-democratic impulse dies hard. A harmony of purposes, ends, virtues, and identities is achievable *only* if we so thoroughly erode the bases of human habits, dispositions, and possibilities as we know and have known them that we willingly engage in radical social surgery. Democrats do not favour wholesale overturnings, in part because the democratic disposition is exquisitely poised between tradition and change, contestation and continuity. The utopian thinker finds democratic fears misplaced, bourgeois temerity, perhaps. Rather, those whose intentions are benign and hearts are pure will surely succeed, one bright day, where others have failed.

Oddly enough, then, it is often anti-democrats who find democracy dull. But for the democrat who is prepared to embrace the give-and-take of democratic political and civic life, it is the utopian who threatens boredom, the tedium of everlasting sameness. The anti-democrat approaches the overgrown democratic garden with its profusion of plants, its weeds and hybrids mixed together, its tendency to stray out of fixed rows and its explosion of colours and aromas, bloomings and wiltings, with an oversize can of weed killer. The democrat takes pleasure in the proliferation. Oh, yes, she weeds and prunes, but she doesn't uproot and refuses to resort to poison. Who knows what might get harmed along with the noxious weeds if one threatens the whole garden with a cure that may do more harm than good? In this garden the humblest daisy and the grandest lily all find their place.

Take something as commonplace and uncontroversial as the vote. For the anti-democrat the vote is either dangerous because the mob can outvote the wise or a bourgeois deception, a ploy, because it means nothing. The vote is an opium of the people. But even democrats are not united in their defence of the vote. Many modern democratic citizens disdain the vote, or hold out little hope for it. They don't think their vote means much. But consider this: suppose a government decided to disenfranchise the citizens of a single state or province as an experiment — to see if the vote was held in as low regard as anti-democrats insist and some democrats bemoan.

It doesn't take much of a stretch of the political imagination to conjure up the explosion — the cries of violation of a basic human right, violation of a constitutional guarantee, denial of democratic equality, creation of a class of subjects with no voice. At that point we would all be reminded of just how vital the vote is to any compelling and coherent notion of the *citizen*. Black slaves in America yearned for the vote as a sign of freedom. Women struggled for it as a form of political recognition, so they, too, could be part of the democratic drama. To be denied the vote is to be denied equal political standing. It is that simple and that important. Writes George Kateb, a political theorist: "Formal membership in constitutional democracy together with the routine workings of the system tends to raise people out of inferior conditions and the internalized sense of inferiority. The coming of constitutional democracy is a liberation, a liberation of mentality and feelings."[49]

But the vote, and other markers of democratic citizenship, have fallen on hard times, criticized as too much of a bad thing. Votes don't matter, power does, and the vote only cajoles us into thinking we have power. Or, on the other hand, votes are too little of a good thing: they may matter, but they don't matter much. Democrats know better.

V

DEMOCRACY'S ENDURING PROMISE

"LET FREEDOM RING!" — the cry of democrats throughout the centuries now echoes round the world. What do aggrieved peoples want? Freedom. When do they want it? Now. That, at least, is the story of the recent past. From Tiananmen Square to Wenceslas Square the rhetoric of protestors, dissidents, and new citizens is cast in the idiom of freedom. But democratic freedom is a very particular sort of freedom, tempered by centuries of hard wisdom that stretches from ancient Attica to the modern Western metropolis, decocted civic lore that tells us that human beings are not only capable of great deeds of courage and selflessness, they are also tempted by power, corrupted by greed, seduced by violence, and weakened by cowardice. It is easy enough to understand why Plato believed, and Aristotle suspected, that human beings were ill-suited to democracy, in large part because they seemed altogether too well suited to licentiousness and anarchy and unscrupulous power-seeking.

Recall, briefly, the generous bounty of troubles I

discussed in earlier chapters: the growth of cynicism and the atrophy of civil society; too much privatizing, acquisitive individualism that translates "wants" into "rights"; an increase in disrespect, even contempt for, the rule-governed practices that make democracy work, from the franchise to due process; a politics of displacement that disdains any distinction between public and private and aims to open up all aspects of life to the harsh glare of publicity; a neglect of practical politics in favour of rageful proclamations of one's unassailable and unassimilable identity as a member of a group; impatience with democratic citizenship and growing enthusiasm for identities based on race, gender, or sexual preference over that of the citizen; a waning of our ability to transmit democratic dispositions and dreams to succeeding generations through education. This is not a pretty picture. It would seem that our prospects are bleak.

Have we, then, lost the *res publica?* Is the drama of democracy in its last act on the stage of the West? Will democratic prospects elsewhere collapse under the weight of nationalism or religious fundamentalism? My answer is a cautious no. Democracy may be in peril, but democracy also remains vibrant and resilient, the great source of political hope in our troubled world. Hope, as Hannah Arendt insisted, is the human capacity that sustains political *being.* Should hopelessness triumph, then and only then will it rightly be said that democracy is forlorn. But that is not where we are at, by no means. The practical realm of democratic civil society, the daily habits that this realm sustains and embodies, may have grown brittle and a bit withered from disuse, but hope remains.

The fact that democracy in its very particular constitutional and representative form is now the dream dreamt by democrats everywhere is, in and of itself, remarkable. For it was not always so. In a 1963 book contrasting the French and American revolutions, Hannah Arendt lamented the fact that it was the French Revolution that young political activists turned to for inspiration rather than the American. Marxists had little use for America's robust yet cautious democrats with their constitutional wrangling and their detailed and very particular Bill of Rights. The French Revolution ended in disaster, bloodshed, and aggressive nationalism. The American Revolution ended in a remarkably steady world of politics without end, a politics resilient enough to withstand the bloodiest civil war the world had known up to that time. But the American Revolution, by contrast to the French, seemed to the reckless and the romantic to lack colour and panache, including the grandiosity of vast lurchings and wrenchings of the sort the French Revolution displayed in full.

Before Arendt penned her elaborate defence of the American revolutionary tradition, Albert Camus had warned about celebrations of the French Revolution, much in vogue in post-World War II Europe, with that revolution recast by Marxists as a class war and a glorious example of justifiable revolutionary violence. Camus cautioned against the mystique of the proletariat, and the attempt by Saint-Just and Robespierre and, later, Marx and Lenin, to fit the world into a theoretical frame that deified a notion of the undivided "will of the people" as a substitution for God himself. Camus excoriated a passion for unity that saw any opposition as treason.

For his efforts Camus was virtually excommunicated from French intellectual life by Sartre and his minions in *Les Temps modernes*.[50] Where Sartre and other latter-day revolutionaries explained away Soviet terror and colluded with reinforcing the power of the state if it was a "people's state," Camus stressed *"le dialogue"* as the form human sociability takes when it appears as politics. Revolutionary politics destroys that sociability, making it impossible to say that "I rebel, therefore we exist." That sounds altogether too moderate if what you want is storming the barricades, terrorizing the bourgeoisie, and taking over the state. That is what revolutionaries seemed to want, proclaiming themselves on the road to a true and perfect democracy by contrast to the paltry, timid form embodied in the American republic.

Camus renounced the claims of politics to aspire to the absolute. Democratic politics must chasten this aspiration, not capitulate to it. For a politics without limits destroys democracy itself. Arendt makes moves similar to Camus's when she distinguishes the rights of freedom and citizenship from the generic "rights of man" proclaimed by the French revolutionaries. Unlike Saint-Just, Robespierre, and the others, the American founders were realists, aware of the fact that human beings will always fall short of some absolute ideal. It follows, according to Arendt, that "the only reasonable hope for salvation from evil and wickedness at which men might arrive even in this world and even by themselves, without any divine assistance," must be the imperfect working of government, the flawed actions of citizens among citizens.[51] Mindful of human limits, the American revolutionaries shored up means to check the urge to unlimited power. Their new government did not promise a future perfect world once all enemies were removed, traitors silenced, and the pure goodness of the people's will articulated; rather, the American democracy held out for a partial redemption only: political hope by contrast to earthly salvation.

Dependent on selectively assimilated memories from antiquity, the French *hommes de lettres* who made the Revolution pursued extreme theoretical abstractions to terrible concrete conclusions. Their "conscious thoughts and words stubbornly returned, again and again, to Roman language, drawn upon to justify revolutionary dictatorship." Oddly the various metaphors "in which the revolution is seen not as the work of men but as an irresistible process, the metaphors of stream and torrent and current, were still coined by the actors themselves, who, however drunk they might have become with the wine of freedom in the abstract, clearly no longer believed that they were free agents," notes Arendt. Prisoners of history, the makers of the French revolution plunged headlong into an orgy of repetitive destruction.

In the twentieth century, when the objective conditions were supposedly ripe for the Bolshevik Revolution, what Lenin and his comrades drew upon was a rhetoric and a historic teleology forged from lessons they claimed they had learned from the French Revolution. The trouble, Arendt claims, was precisely this: "those who went into the school of revolution learned and knew beforehand the course a revolution must take." It must defeat open opponents. Then it must ferret out and destroy hidden enemies. To do this it must centralize power, enhance the police, create a layer of spies and functionaries. It must liquidate hypocrites. Finally it must forfeit some of its own. This is a "grandiose ludicrousness," Arendt avers, for its automatic adherence to the claims of revolutionary necessity is compulsive and robotic, unlike the uncoerced actions and reactions of free citizens doing the work of practical politics.

Arendt also taxes the French revolutionaries for the way they promised to solve the social question, problems of poverty and misery. It worked in the following manner. The people were deemed abject and silent by definition. They required spokesmen and champions. But having construed the problems the Revolution was meant to solve in nigh-eschatalogical terms, the dynamic set in motion restlessly sought targets for correction, reproof, or extinction. Absolute ends require means without limit. Revolutionary pity is boundless in its bathetic force so long as the suffering are faceless, a mass. Distinguishing this abstract pity from genuine compassion, Arendt writes: "For compassion, to be stricken with the suffering of someone else as though it were contagious, and pity, to be sorry without being touched in the flesh, are not only not the same, they may not even be related." One feels compassion, or comprehends it, only in and through the particular. The moment one generalizes, this specificity is lost and boundless pity comes into play: hence Robespierre's glorification of the poor.

Pity *for* is not the same as solidarity *with*. Those who pity without limit develop a thirst for power and gain "a vested interest in the existence of the weak." Abstract pity invites cheap sentiment and confounds any possibility for genuine political freedom. "Since the days of the French Revolution," writes Arendt, "it has been the boundlessness of their sentiments that made revolutionaries so curiously insensitive to reality in general and to the reality of persons in particular, whom they felt no compunctions in sacrificing to their 'principles,' or to the course of history, or to the cause of revolution as such." Virtue without limits is evil. The real poor, in their human distinctness, are lost.

To say that all power resides in the people and that the people are all who suffer is to understand power as a kind of natural, pre-political force. In contrast, by distinguishing violence from authentic power, the American rebels rejected the notion of irrefutable necessity and the need for force, believing instead, in Arendt's words, that power comes into being when "people . . . get together and bind themselves through promises, covenants, and mutual pledges;

only such power, which rests on reciprocity and mutuality, was real power and legitimate . . ." The American revolutionaries at least appreciated this grammar of action, the action of citizens in their plurality, not a mass in its anonymity.

Political power doesn't grow out of the barrel of a gun, or flow from the dripping blade of the guillotine. Rather, it comes into being, it makes its appearance, when men and women, acting in common as citizens, get together and find a way to express their collective hopes and possibilities. Consider the American Civil Rights Movement of the 1960s. There are observers that fault civil rights activists for doing too much — taking to the streets, boycotts, and mass demonstrations seem uncivil to them — or for doing too little: refusing to attack whites, or refraining from admitting forthrightly that, "This is about power, pure and simple. Whites have it; blacks don't; we want it." But narrowly juridical treatments of the civil rights struggle miss the boat — it was about laws, yes, but it was about much more than legal change.

A modulated politics whose practitioners opened their hands in gestures of anticipated fellowship to all persons of goodwill, white or black, rich or poor, offends those who want a totalistic and revolutionary politics. Hate is easy; arousing the regressive urges of one's fellow men and women requires little more than a capacity for spite. What is difficult, what is the most daunting task of the political imagination, is to fight the allure of hate, particularly when it comes to us in the name of revolution.

Martin Luther King understood this. He knew very well what an experience of "the political" was all about and how it rested uneasily within the confines of a wizened conventional politics of mere proceduralism, on the one hand, yet stood as an alternative to a politics of revolutionary violence, on the other. A recent historian, Richard King, talks of the "repertory of freedom" embraced by the civil rights movement. He observes that freedom in Western political thinking involves at least four basic meanings: legal freedom, freedom as autonomy, participatory freedom, and freedom as collective deliverance from a subjugated condition. Here once again Arendt's insistence that political freedom is public, open, and involves action helps one to appreciate the hope embraced by, and expressed in, the identities and actions of civil rights citizens, those tens of thousands of ordinary folks who found within themselves the courage to act in behalf of each "I" and in so doing helped to create a "we." Protestors did not seek pity; they were not Robespierre's abject, silent mass. They did, however, embrace a politics of compassion that could draw out from others a spirit of renewed hopefulness and commitment.

The action of a free citizen is not just any form of movement or behaviour; rather, rooted in hope, such action marks new beginnings, generates possibilities that once seemed foreclosed. Thus, "Like most great movements of historical change the civil rights movement was a great surprise," notes King.[52] As I already suggested, the politics of civil

rights cannot be confined within the primacy of
self-interest, as many contemporary political scientists claim. They spin out their own version of cynicism in advocating so-called rational choice theory,
a formula that reduces citizens first, last, and always
to calculators of marginal utility. It is not that civil
rights citizens denied such motives altogether. But
a politics of self-interest captures only one moment,
and not the most important at that, of the rich idea
of freedom animating King and his cohorts. Freedom as collective liberation from bondage, throwing off the nonrecognition lodged in a denial of the
dignity of rights-based citizenship, was vital.
Equally important was the "necessary transformation of the self experienced by those actively engaged in direct action" as free citizens.[53] To see such
solidaristic freedom and self-transformation as
merely peripheral to "the explicit goals of liquida-
tion of racial segregation and black disenfranchise-
ment" is to lose the ethical power and historic
complexity of the civil rights struggle.

Civil rights protestors, like the Athenians gathered to hear Pericles extol the glory of their city and
remind them of why she was worthy of their sacrifice, shared a repertoire of beliefs and ideals. They
recognized that powerful ethical convictions are
fungible in a democratic culture — they can be
turned to transformative civic purposes. The freedom they yearned for flows from the lexicon of
liberty and political equality. But it certainly owes a
great deal, as well, to the conviction that every person is unique and irreplaceable, a child of God. The

Christian's biblically grounded belief in the equal worth of all souls in the eyes of God profoundly transformed received notions of political equality, putting the stress on human dignity by contrast to equal power to rule and to be ruled.

As encoded in law, democratic rights make reference to this idea of a dignified individual. Although Americans sometimes grow weary of "rights talk" — as I indicated in a previous chapter, just about anything anybody wants gets bruited about as a right in America nowadays — it remains the case that rights as immunities, as the way we express what governments are not permitted to do to us because we are persons with political standing and human dignity, is both a precious reality and a precarious achievement. For the vast majority of the world's people, "human rights" is the name they give to a persistent yearning. These are lessons I learned or, perhaps better put, came to remember as I listened to the powerful and terrible stories told me by mothers who have become public citizens — in Argentina, Central America, Israel and the West Bank, the Czech Republic, and the United States. Because it was the stories of those "political Mothers" called *las madres*, the Mothers of the Disappeared, that I heard first and that jolted me out of my own complacency about rights and public freedom, it is their saga I will recount briefly. The Mothers of the Disappeared are Argentine mothers of sons and daughters who were "disappeared" in the terrible years of Argentina's so-called Dirty War, from 1976 to 1982 when Argentina was ruled by three successive military juntas. To be a *desaparecido*, a "disappeared," is to be abducted, usually tortured, before being killed and buried anonymously.

As backdrop to the story of *las madres*, it might be useful for me to indicate what I brought to the hearing, recording, and interpretation of the Mothers' tales of grief and defiance. In a 1982 essay, "Antigone's Daughters," I recalled the transgressive words and deeds of Antigone as worthy of consideration by contemporary feminists skeptical of state-dominated politics and determined to position themselves against a public identity subsumed entirely within the extant terms of a juridical notion of the citizen and a self-interested notion of politics. I recalled Antigone and her defiance of Creon, King of Thebes and her own uncle, when he denies burial honours to Antigone's slain brother and Creon's nephew, Polynices, a traitor to the city.

I cannot here repeat the many themes I found in the play that seemed an appropriate feminist parable for our own time. Primarily I wanted to show that conflicts between duty to family and the requirements of civic order are not so easily resolved. Private life and public life alike suffer if one gives everything over to a single sphere or dimension. As well, I was unconvinced by the "oppressed group model," analyses that saw in women's traditional identities only victimization, thereby denying women historic agency and authority. Those who accepted this view found themselves celebrating the statuses and identities of successful and dominant males — an unwittingly ironic posture for a feminist,

I thought. The critical point was my insistence that to construe the careerist public world as the only sphere within which individuals made choices, exercised power, or had control meant that the private world remained shrouded in a presumably unchosen, unthinking condition of mere necessity. As well, democratic politics got reduced to a vehicle aimed at securing one's private ambitions.

Positioning women as social actors in the world, I aimed to pit them against imperious public power and petty private demands, even as they struggled to sustain public identities as citizens and embraced worlds of intimate obligation and promise. Both worlds, public and private, are social locations. Breaking out of a rigid public-private dichotomy, but recognizing and seeking to preserve some version of a public-private distinction, is a complex task but a necessary one. Or so I claimed.

Jane Addams, a great American public citizen and social thinker, is usefully drawn into the story at this point. In one of her early essays, "Filial Relations," which appeared in a collection called *Democracy and Social Ethics,* Addams described the conflict between familial duties and dependencies and the responsibilities of the individual to the larger social whole. She saw this conflict as necessary and sometimes tragic. "The collision of interests, each of which has a real moral basis and a right to its own place in life, is bound to be more or less tragic. It is the struggle between two claims, the destruction of either of which would bring ruin to ethical life."[54]

Addams understood that women could not

ongoingly play out the drama of ethical life in the private sphere or family alone. Addams raises to an explicit concern questions of female identity and political purpose. Women, too, must undergo a struggle for identity and recognition. The family claim *is* a claim: we are duty-bound to answer. But it is not the only claim and cannot absorb the whole of us. We must hold in fruitful tension the "I" of the self, the "us" and "ours" of the family, and the "we of citizens" of the wider democratic civic world. No theoretical abstraction has authenticity, she argued, unless it is rooted in the concrete human experiences of familial and wider social claims. That is one of democracy's enduring promises.

What Addams is about is something quite different from those preaching and practising a politics of displacement of the sort I criticized in an earlier chapter. For Addams it is clear that, when one enters the public world, one has to make one's case in a shared political idiom: we are not little epistemological isolates, stripped-down Robinson Crusoe monads. Let us hold these recognitions in mind as I return to the story of the Mothers' tragedy and how they took to the public square, speaking a double language of maternal grief and human rights, advocating justice and seeking recognition not so much for themselves but for the "disappeared." The Mothers transgressed the boundary between private and public in order to reaffirm the integrity of that boundary against those who, in the name of the state, had violated it by rounding up, torturing, and killing thousands of persons, most of them young, and all of them stripped of dignity and denied political standing and recognition.

The authoritarian, militarist system the Mothers opposed, after it had seized and destroyed their children, permitted one sort of politics (or pseudo-politics) only — a politics of supplication to high authorities. All of political life was constructed vertically. But another possibility — essential to any democratic political life — had been virtually wiped out. Some have called this the "horizontal voice."[55] By this they mean the right to address others, to call forth some sort of "we," to make manifest a political identity. It is this "horizontal voice" that anti-democratic regimes must try to destroy, yet it is precisely this voice the Mothers found in themselves. They created a "we," they forged a group political identity on the basis of their shared experience. Condemned to silence, they repudiated the sentence of the regime, took to a great public square in Buenos Aires, the Plaza de Mayo, and voiced their grief and their outrage. Having lived a private life of grief, they found strength and political identity by deprivatizing their mourning; in fusing a language of grief with a language of human rights, they kept alive the particular realities and identities of individuals, their sons and daughters, tormented and lost to state terror, but they also issued a call to nonviolent arms to their fellow Argentines and to the wider world. Reclaim human dignity! they cried. Reclaim the birthright of free citizens! Protect Mothers and Families, yes, but embrace and protect a democratic constitution, as well.

Recall, if you will, the potent terms moving through this discussion thus far: hope and reality. Hope as that which gives rise to political being and action, for without hope the people, and individuals, perish politically. But reality, too, concrete attention to particular concerns by contrast to grandiose schemes that require anti-democratic methods in order to attain some ostensibly better or more perfect democracy — down the road a piece, after we have rid ourselves of counterrevolutionaries, of all who stand in our way. In my conversations with the Mothers, stretching over nearly a decade, I was struck by how many of them understood the language of rights in its fullest and richest embodiment as setting boundaries not only to the politics of the state but to their own politics. "We, too, must behave democratically in our movement," one Mother told me, "if we are to advocate democracy for our society."

To be sure, human rights language is scarcely so ancient a maternal language as that of mourning and loss. The mothers put these languages together. Human rights was, for them, a way to express the timeless immunities of persons from the depredations of their governments rather than as a vehicle for entitlements, as we Americans more and more see things. Rights gave political form and shape to their disobedience, linking them to an international network of associations. They not only breached the private-public divide of their own society in the interest of protecting the integrity of family life against wholesale destruction and definition by government, but crossed the boundaries of states, as well, astonishing themselves in the process as they gained support and inspired other human-rights-based Mothers' movements throughout Central and Latin America.

The Mothers made it very clear to me that they sought justice, not vengeance. They opposed the death penalty. "Human beings are not robots," Renée Epelbaum, mother of three *desaparecidos,* told me. "The man or people who killed my children are criminals, those who tortured and those who gave the order to torture. Human beings are responsible for what they do. They destroyed the rights, the lives, of other human beings." Maria Adela Antokoletz added: "When justice is not fulfilled, when rights are not cherished, democratic possibilities vanish." Renée sadly continued: "You know, we understand that not everyone responsible can be punished — that's utopian. But we must press forward from a sense of hope and reality. We don't want the Mothers movement changed into a class movement. We demand justice strongly. But we are not utopians." Maria Adela: "What we want and think is that the Mothers of the Plaza de Mayo must endure forever, much more than in our own lifetimes. It has to do with having a guardian position in society in order to watch so this will not happen again."

These brave Mothers encoded democracy in its specifically liberal and constitutional understandings, grounded in human rights construed as immunities and duties, into their political self-definition. Through their actions and deeds the ethical force of an argument from human rights helped to animate quiescent sectors of a moribund and demoralized Argentine civil society. Whatever Argentina's future fate, these Mothers would say, human rights can never again be trampled upon with such impunity. That is their wager — one to which they have devoted their lives in the name of the lost lives of their children.

Faced with such stories, how can we citizens of relatively secure, ordered, and well-established democracies lose heart? The Mothers did not see themselves as heroes. "We have been courageous, that is true. We have always acted with dignity. But we did it because of our children. We *had* to do it." This stress on a simple moral imperative — we had to do it — is typical of stories of democratic courage and perseverance. "We" had to, "I" had to, not because it was mandated, not because it was in conformity with what had been drilled into me through years of martial severity, as in Sparta, but because *I* had to. We hold these truths to be self-evident, I hear echoing in the backdrop to such affirmations of the burdens of free responsibility.

A remarkable freedom from bitterness and rancour, from the corrosive force of resentment, characterizes these brave democratic exemplars. The issue, remember, is democratic possibility and the robustness of democratic yearning in our complex world as it lurches and lumbers toward the end of the twentieth century. I want to suggest that political actors all over the world are busy writing new acts for, and enacting scenes from, an ongoing drama of democracy, often as a form of dissent and disaffection from an undemocratic order.

Take a rather different example, Václav Havel, who showed as much courage as the Mothers when he found himself, on several occasions, in Communist prisons for his dissident crimes. But even in rebellion, Havel insists, there must be limits. Freedom is not the working out of a foreordained teleology of self-realization or political prophecy; rather, freedom comes from embracing that which it is given one to do in one's own time and place. Democracy is the political form that enables human beings to work out freedom as responsibility, in service to the notion that there are things worth suffering for. Note the distinction here: one may accept, as the burden of free responsibility, suffering from prison or torture. But one does not mandate suffering for others and one does not feel a wholly abstract pity toward those who suffer.

For Havel, hope, responsibility, freedom, acceptance of paradox are all of a piece. What makes Havel such a fascinating performer of democratic political thought is that, from a stance of compassion rather than sickly pity, he provokes the complacent, mocks the smug, tweaks the arrogant, and suffers without excusing the weak. In his rejection of the petrified politics deeded us by the legacy of the French Revolution and a century of total wars, Havel helps us to move into the future disillusioned hence paradoxically free. I think he would agree that a central task of political philosophy for our time lies in recognizing, for what it is, what has happened in

Europe since 1989. What has happened is the definitive collapse of an attempt to rebuild human society on some overarching *Weltanschauung*. Europe, Havel noted, has entered the long tunnel at the end of the light. This is a wonderful metaphor for the democratic drama more generally. There is the light — the glorious light of public freedom, individual liberty, and political equality — and then we move through that long tunnel, a world of politics without end.

Havel's arguments continue in this vein: the world is possible only because we are grounded. If this world of "personal responsibility," with its characteristic virtues and marks of decency, both public and private (justice, honour, friendship, fidelity), is ruptured or emptied, what rushes in to take its place is politics as a "rational technology of power" whose exemplar is the manager, the apparatchik. Humans play God and the wreckage grows. Man finds himself in the "rut of totalitarian thought, where he is not his own and where he surrenders his own reason and conscience . . ."[56] Man lives within a lie; he gives himself over to the "social auto-totality" and he or she who does so surrenders identity and responsibility falters. The totalitarian society counts on this and requires it. The democratic society, in its mass, consumerist forms, may give rise to a similar *mentalité*, and should this grow apace, shared responsibility for the civic world will fade there, too.

Well, we have come rather far — from Pericles' Athens to Havel's Czech Republic, from the Mothers of the Disappeared to American civil rights protestors, from counsels of cynicism and a politics of resentment, to a politics of hope and reality. Perhaps I may introduce just one more theme — our ongoing dialogue with the dead. In anti-democratic societies, whether a twentieth-century totalitarian or bureaucratic authoritarian state or, further back, in revolutionary cataclysms of the French sort, one's ancestors are pretty much reviled and repudiated. We are starting brand-new, anti-democrats proclaim. We will not be bound by the past with its petty and benighted ways.

I recall a stroll in a lovely town in France's Berry region with good friends of mine several summers ago. With one of these friends I entered a Romanesque church dating, I believe, from the ninth or tenth century. I noticed that a number of the sarcophagi offered a curious spectacle — the heads of saints and angels and other representations of venerated persons had been lopped off. I looked around and found that all sorts of lovely if, by now, somewhat decrepit statues and figures had been beheaded. Being an American, I thought of youthful vandalism on a drunken Saturday night. But I asked my friend, "Who did this? Who would do a thing like this?"

He answered matter-of-factly, "Revolutionaries."

These defaced relics had fallen prey to eighteenth-century political zeal. It was a breathtakingly simple response, and it reminded me, once again, of why I am not a revolutionary convinced that I have the right to destroy that which others, past and present, hold dear.

In America today we hear pitiless assaults on the past: all was oppression and domination and racist

or sexist horror. But what happens to our obligation
to the dead? Are we modern democrats not thus
obliged? Wholesale assaults on the past enjoin and
legitimate a vulgar willfulness of the present moment. That is not what the drama of democracy is
all about. Rather, it is about permanent contestation
between conservation and change, between tradition and transformation. To jettison one side is to live
either in a sterile present-mindedness or an equally
sterile reaction. Let me offer as an example of what
I have in mind a passage from a novel by the great
American writer Willa Cather. The novel in question
is called *A Lost Lady*. Cather's protagonist, Neil Herbert, discovers the classics and the classics provide
him a way into a new world and a way out of the
town of Sweetwater, Nebraska. Cather describes
Neil Herbert's discovery of the past, the past of his
own culture:

> There were philosophical works in the collection but
> he did no more than open and glance at them. He
> had no curiosity about what men had thought, but
> about what they had felt and lived he had a great
> deal. If anyone had told him these were classics and
> represented the wisdom of the ages, he would
> doubtless have let them alone. He did not think of
> these books as something invented to beguile the
> idle hour, but as living creatures caught in the very
> behavior of living, surprised behind their
> misleading severity of form and phrase. He was
> eavesdropping upon the past, being let into the
> great world that had plunged and littered and

sumptuously sinned long before little western towns
were dreamed of. Those rapt evenings beside the
lamp gave him a long perspective, including his
conception of the people about him, made him
know just what he wished his own relations with
these people to be.

In novels Herbert finds a living, breathing, socially embodied tradition. This is the excitement I
hope to convey — I hope I have conveyed — about
the drama of democracy. For democracy invites us
into the complexities and possibilities of a heady
tradition. We are always part of a tradition or part
of the fragments of many traditions. There is no
point denying this fact: that will not make it so. As
Arendt taught us, the French revolutionaries who
fancied themselves untrammelled as they proposed
to uproot one world utterly and create another totally were, in fact, drearily stuck in the dead hand of
a teleology of historic necessity. A tradition with
many voices — and that is the democratic tradition — leads us out of ourselves, out of previously
unthought perspectives into worlds at once more
self-aware and less predictable. To think a tradition
is to bring matters to the surface, to engage with
interlocutors long dead, protagonists who never
lived save on the page, and through that engagement to elaborate alternative conceptions through
which to apprehend one's world and the way that
world represents itself.

"Home is where one starts from," writes T. S. Eliot
in his poem "East Coker," but, the poet goes on,

"As we grow older / The world becomes stranger, the pattern more complicated / Of dead and living." Faithfulness to this complexity without slavish adherence to the past, including our own and that of our society, that, too, is central to an enduring democratic promise. *But above all, be not afraid,* our democratic forefathers and foremothers would tell us. Democracy is an unpredictable enterprise. Our patience with its ups and downs, its debates and compromises, its very anti-authoritarianism, may wane as we become inured to more and more control — all in the name of freedom. We must be on guard.

The task of the democratic political imagination is possible if civility is not utterly destroyed, if room remains for playful experimentation from deep seriousness of purpose free from totalistic intrusion and ideological control.[57] For even when equality and justice seem far-off ideals, freedom preserves the human discourse necessary to work toward the realization of both. One day as our children or their children or their children's children stroll in gardens, debate in public places, or poke through the ashes of a wrecked civilization, they may not rise to call us blessed. But neither will they curse our memory because we permitted, through our silence, democracy to pass away as in a dream.

NOTES

1. E. J. Dionne, *Why Americans Hate Politics* (New York: Simon and Schuster, 1991).

2. Thomas Byrne Edsall, with Mary D. Edsall, *Chain Reaction* (New York: Norton, 1991).

3. See Ralph Ketcham, ed., *The Anti-Federalist Papers and the Constitutional Convention Debates* (New York: New American Library, 1986) 18.

4. Alexis de Tocqueville, *Democracy in America*, trans. Henry Reeve, rev. Francis Bowed, ed. Phillips Bradley (New York: Vintage, 1945) 2:293.

5. George Kateb celebrates our individualism and finds our worries excessive. The words in quotes are drawn from his *The Inner Ocean* (Ithaca, NY: Cornell UP, 1992) 31.

6. Pope John Paul II, "Sollicitudo Rei Socialis," *Origins* 17 (March 13, 1988) 33:650.

7. Pope John Paul II 654–655.

8. Alan Wolfe, *Whose Keeper? Social Science and Moral Obligation* (Berkeley: University of California Press, 1989) 2.

9. Mary Ann Glendon, *Rights Talk* (New York: Free Press, 1992).

10. Glendon 20.

11. Glendon 30.

12. Kateb 103–104.

13. Charles Taylor, *The Malaise of Modernity* (Concord, ON: House of Anansi Press, 1991) 117.

14. James Q. Wilson, "The Government Gap," *The New Republic* (June 3, 1991) 38.

15. Cited in Elizabeth Mensch and Alan Freeman, *The Politics of Virtue* (Durham, NC: Duke UP, 1993) 128.

16. I first articulated concern about a politics of displacement in my *Public Man, Private Woman: Women in Social and Political Thought* (Princeton: Princeton UP, 1981, 2nd ed. 1993).

17. Sheldon Wolin, "Democracy, Difference and Recognition," *Political Theory* 21 (August 1993) 3:468.

18. Milan Kundera, "In Defense of Intimacy," an interview with Philip Roth, *The Village Voice* (June 26, 1984) 42.

19. There is something of a paradox here, of course, for egalitarian feminists who respect some public-private distinction challenge the whole concept of "protection" and the ideology behind it. Radical feminists, at least to certain ends and purposes, endorse a sweeping affirmation of the notion. My reference point in this discussion is one of the standard feminist works on the sub-

ject of battered women, Susan Schechter's *Women and Male Violence: The Visions and Struggles of the Battered Women's Movement* (Boston: South End Press, 1982). The subtitle alone — "Visions and Struggles" — locates the reader as one who is either with or against the project; either struggling for or blocking the way to a new world (emphases mine).

20. Schechter 239.

21. Schechter 271.

22. A full version of my critical examination of gay liberationist ideology is available in my piece, "The Paradox of Gay Liberation," *Salmangundi* (Fall 1982–Winter 1983) 250–280.

23. "The Paradox of Gay Liberation," 257, 263. The citations are drawn from several 1970s gay liberationist texts that helped to frame the subsequent debate and continue to mark the distinction between civil rights and liberationist politics.

24. Isaiah Berlin, *The Crooked Timber of Humanity* (New York: Vintage, 1992) 32, 47.

25. Charles Taylor, *Multiculturalism and the Politics of Recognition* (Princeton: Princeton UP, 1992) 34.

26. Kurt Vonnegut, Jr., *Welcome to the Monkey House* (New York: Delacorte Press, 1968) 7.

27. Richard Rodriguez, *Hunger of Memory. The Education of Richard Rodriguez* (Boston: David R. Godine, 1981) 154–55.

28. Kateb 23–24.

29. Wolin 466.

30. Wolin 476.

31. Wolin 480.

32. Michael Oakeshott, *The Voice of Liberal Learning* (New Haven: Yale UP, 1989) 38–39.

33. Oakeshott 29.

34. From Havel's essay, "Power and Powerlessness," in *Living in Truth* (London: Faber and Faber, 1987) 104.

35. A brief but helpful summary of various uses and definitions of democracy, past and present, may be found in Noberto Bobbio, *Democracy and Dictatorship* (Minneapolis: University of Minnesota Press, 1989). For a fully fleshed-out discussion of Plato's anti-democratic suspicions see my *Public Man, Private Woman: Women in Social and Political Thought*.

36. Hannah Arendt is perhaps the most enthusiastic celebrant of ancient freedom and the glory of word and deed made possible only in the political realm of the *polis*. See her panegyric to this lost world in *The Human Condition* (Chicago: University of Chicago Press, 1958).

37. Nicole Loraux, *Inventing Athens: The Funeral Oration in the Classical City* (Cambridge, MA: Harvard UP, 1986) 202.

38. Thucydides, *History of the Peloponnesian War*, trans. Rex Warner (New York: Penguin, 1988) 143–151.

39. Loraux 175.

40. Abraham Lincoln, *Lincoln: Speeches, Letters, Miscellaneous Writings, The Lincoln–Douglas Debates, 1832–1858* (New York: The Library of America, 1989) 484.

41. From Book VIII of Plato's *The Republic*, trans. Allan Bloom (New York: Basic Books, 1968) 239.

42. Plato, *Gorgias*, trans. Walter Hamilton (New York: Penguin, 1971) 44.

43. *The Republic*, Book VI, 496–498.

44. *The Republic*, Book VI, 500–501.

45. The *locus classicus* of Aristotle on political forms is, of course, his *Politics*, trans. Ernest Barker (New York: Oxford UP, 1962).

46. Thomas Hobbes, *The Leviathan* (New York: Penguin, 1968) 227, 236.

47. Cited in Mary Midgley, *Wickedness: A Philosophical Essay* (London: Routledge and Kegan Paul, 1984) 195.

48. Isaiah Berlin, *The Crooked Timber of Humanity* 20–21.

49. Kateb 26.

50. See Albert Camus, *The Rebel* (New York: Knopf, 1954).

51. Hannah Arendt, *On Revolution* (New York: Penguin, 1963). All Arendt citations are drawn, variously, from this single text.

52. Richard H. King, *Civil Rights and the Idea of Freedom* (Oxford: Oxford UP, 1992) 28.

53. King 100.

54. Jane Addams, *Democracy and Social Ethics* (New York: Macmillan, 1902) 76–77.

55. This is an argument elaborated by Guillermo O'Donnell and based on the concepts of Albert O. Hirschman in his book, *Exit, Voice, and Loyalty*. (Cambridge, MA: Harvard UP, 1970). O'Donnell's essay appears in "Shifting Involvements: Reflections from the Recent Argentine Experience," Kellogg Institute Working Paper 58 (February 1986) Notre Dame University.

56. From "Politics and Conscience" in *Living in Truth* 151.

57. I should note that this final paragraph is drawn from the conclusion of chapter 7 in the first edition of my book *Public Man, Private Woman: Women in Social and Political Thought*. I have always been particularly fond of these few sentences and, as no one else appears to have cited them, the task fell to me.

The CBC Massey Lectures Series

Gregory Baum	Compassion and Solidarity: The Church for Others	0-88794-3357
Stafford Beer	Designing Freedom	0-88794-0757
Noam Chomsky	Necessary Illusions: Thought Control in Democratic Societies	0-88784-5193
Ursula Franklin	The Real World of Technology	0-88794-3756
Northrop Frye	The Educated Imagination	0-88794-0390
Carlos Fuentes	Latin America: At War with the Past	0-88794-146X
Robert Heilbroner	Twenty-first Century Capitalism	0-88784-5347
R.D. Laing	The Politics of the Family	0-88794-0285
Doris Lessing	Prisons We Choose to Live Inside	0-88784-5215
R.C. Lewontin	Biology as Ideology	0-88784-5185
C.B. Macpherson	The Real World of Democracy	0-88794-0013
George Steiner	Nostalgia for the Absolute	0-88794-0765
Charles Taylor	The Malaise of Modernity	0-88784-5207